THE LIFE AND TIMES OF
SHERLOCK HOLMES

THE LIFE AND TIMES OF
SHERLOCK HOLMES

PHILIP WELLER
with
Christopher Roden

STUDIO EDITIONS
London

This edition published 1992 by Studio Editions Ltd.,
Princess House, 50 Eastcastle Street, London W1N 7AP, England.

Copyright this edition © Studio Editions Ltd., 1992.

Designed and edited by Anness Publishing,
4a The Old Forge, 7 Caledonian Road,
London N1 9DX.

Designer: Adrian Waddington
Watermark Communications Group Ltd.,
Chesham, England.

ISBN 1-85170-722-0

Printed and bound in Singapore

CONTENTS

PREFACE

It has reasonably been claimed that more foreign visitors to London know the address of Sherlock Holmes than know that of the Prime Minister: yet Sherlock Holmes never existed. The current occupants of Sherlock Holmes's famous address, the Abbey National bank, receive thousands of letters for Sherlock Holmes every year and have to employ a secretary to deal with his correspondence: yet Sherlock Holmes never existed. Respected pillars of society around the world spend countless hours examining every aspect of Sherlock Holmes's life: yet Sherlock Holmes never existed. What is the fascination which this apparently fictional character holds, and has held for many decades, for those who are his dedicated followers? No-one has ever produced a single, satisfactory answer to that question, but this book will attempt to explore the areas from which that fascination grows. The authors of this book invite you to join them in an exploration of the land where Sherlock Holmes still lives, a place where it is always 1895, and a place where, to paraphrase the words used by Holmes in calling Doctor John H. Watson to embark on yet another adventure:

"The Game Is Still Afoot."

THE LIFE AND TIMES OF SHERLOCK HOLMES

THE LEGENDARY
MR HOLMES

The Birth of the Great Detective

In 1882 a physician of Irish descent and Scottish birth set up his first independent practice in the genteel seaside resort of Southsea in Hampshire. The practice was slow to grow, and to while away the hours this young doctor began to develop his interest in the writing of adventure stories. During March and April of 1886 he produced a story with a completely new type of lead character: a private, consulting detective who produced amazing results through the application of a keen, analytical mind to the careful observation of the clues available. It was thus that Sherlock Holmes first saw the light of day, and the delivery was performed by Doctor Arthur Conan Doyle.

The first Holmesian appearance was in an adventure called *A Study in Scarlet*. This is one of the four Holmes long stories, and it was never to be a financial success for Doyle. He tried various publishers and received numerous rejections before he finally accepted the princely sum of £25, offered by Ward Lock, for the total rights to the story. Even then, the publishers managed to include an implied insult with their offer, in mentioning that: "We could not publish it this year as the market is flooded at present with cheap fiction . . ." The story appeared the following year, in November 1887, as part of a magazine called *Beeton's Christmas Annual*, produced by the brother of the more famous cookery book author. Doyle later remarked that he never received a further penny from the story, but such are the changes in values that a mint copy of that one-shilling magazine would now sell for many tens of thousands of pounds, and the manuscripts of some of his shorter stories have sold for six-figure sums.

The Early Growth of Sherlock Holmes

A Study in Scarlet provided an excellent introduction to Sherlock Holmes and to his colleague and biographer Doctor Watson, as well as to the then revolutionary forensic

FIRST EDITION OF *A STUDY IN SCARLET (above). The book, published in 1888, was illustrated by Charles Altamont Doyle, the author's father.*

DR JOSEPH BELL *(left), Conan Doyle's professor of medicine at Edinburgh University and the original inspiration for the sleuth of Baker Street.*

WILLIAM GILLETTE AS SHERLOCK HOLMES *(opposite). Illustration of the renowned actor from a 1907 issue of* Vanity Fair. *The artist was Leslie Ward, better known as "Spy".*

SECOND EDITION OF *A STUDY IN SCARLET*, 1891 *(above)*. *Illustrated by George Hutchinson.*

THE SIGN OF FOUR (right). The second edition, 1892.

THE SIGN OF THE FOUR (far right) was the second Holmes story to appear and was featured in Lippincott's Monthly Magazine, *February 1890.*

FIRST EDITION OF *THE ADVENTURES OF SHERLOCK HOLMES*, 1892 *(below)*. *Illustrated by Sidney Paget.*

THE SIGN OF FOUR, 1902 (below right). Souvenir edition.

THE FIRST BOOK EDITION OF *THE SIGN OF FOUR*, 1890 *(below far right). Conan Doyle had the title shortened for the book.*

This Number Contains a Complete Story,

THE SIGN OF THE FOUR

BY A. CONAN DOYLE.

FEBRUARY, 1890.

LIPPINCOTT'S

MONTHLY MAGAZINE.

CONTENTS.

		PAGE
THE SIGN OF THE FOUR	A. Conan Doyle	147—223
(With a full-page Illustration.)		
NATHANIEL HAWTHORNE'S "ELIXIR OF LIFE"	Julian Hawthorne	224
WHY DO WE MEASURE MANKIND?	Francis Galton, F.R.S.	236
BOMBIN (Poem)	Daniel L. Dawson	241
THE SALON IDEA IN NEW YORK	C. H. Crandall	243
VALENTINE (Poem)	Margaret H. Lawless	253
SHELLEY'S WELSH HAUNTS	Professor C. H. Herford	254
THE BLUE-AND-GOLD MAN-CHILD	M. H. Catherwood	258
THE NEWSPAPER AND THE INDIVIDUAL; A Plea for Press Censorship	A. E. Watrous	267
A DEAD MAN'S DIARY I.—IV.		271
WHAT DID OUR FOREFATHERS MEAN BY RENT?	Rev. W. Cunningham, D.D. D.Sc.	278
MARRIED GENIUSES	John Habberton	283
IS ENGLISH FICTION NARROW?	John A. Steuart	287

PRICE ONE SHILLING.

London : WARD, LOCK AND CO., Salisbury Square, E.C.
Philadelphia : J. B. LIPPINCOTT Co.

All rights reserved.]

methodology which Holmes uses. This story was to form a good basis for those which followed, although it will be seen that some of the later stories include details which clash with those in the original narrative. The stories were never seen as great literature by Doyle, and his annoyance with his public's almost total preoccupation with Holmes later decided him to kill off the character. Initially, however, he saw the popularity of his new creation as a means towards being able to devote more time to "serious" writing.

In August 1889, at a dinner given by J.M. Stoddart, a literary agent for the American *Lippincott's Monthly Magazine*, Oscar Wilde and Conan Doyle were encouraged to produce new novels. The results were Oscar Wilde's famous *The Picture of Dorian Gray* and the second Holmes long story *The Sign of the Four*. The latter was the original title of the story, but Doyle shortly afterwards decided that he preferred the shorter title *The Sign of Four*, which is how it is usually known now. He produced the book in only six weeks.

Doyle moved from Southsea to central London in 1890 to specialize as an oculist, but this practice met with a similar lack of success and he found even more time for his writings. He began to produce the twelve immortal stories which were later combined as *The Adventures of Sherlock Holmes*, a volume containing many of the most popular of the short stories.

July 1891 saw the beginning of an extremely successful series of collaborations, with these new Holmes short stories being published in the monthly *The Strand Magazine* and accompanied by the illustrations of Sidney Paget. The commission for the illustrations was originally meant for Sidney's brother, Walter, but was mistakenly sent to

Sidney, who used Walter as his model. The Paget portraits were to fix the physical image of Holmes almost indelibly in the minds of many British readers. In America, however, the Holmesian image has been more closely associated with the later illustrations of Frederic Dorr Steele in *Collier's* magazine. From the often Samurai-like portraits of Holmes in many Japanese publications, it appears that Holmes is able to be all things to all nations.

The "Death" of Sherlock Holmes

In the summer of 1892, Doyle began producing the next thirteen short stories, twelve of which were later to become *The Memoirs of Sherlock Holmes*, for *The Strand Magazine*. Only a year later, however, he had already decided to end the life of the character he considered to be from "a lower stratum of literary achievement". In the Christmas 1893 issue of *The Strand Magazine*, the public was devastated to read of the death of Sherlock Holmes at the Reichenbach Falls in Switzerland, in *The Final Problem*. City gentlemen in London wore black armbands, and Doyle received threats and letters of abuse. In spite of his poor opinion of the Holmes stories, Doyle did take note of the feelings which others had for the

character, but it was not until 1901 that he was to give way to pressures for more narratives about Holmes.

The initial result of Doyle's change of heart was the greatest of the long Holmes stories: a Holmes adventure from before his "demise", *The Hound of the Baskervilles*. It was here that the Holmes phenomenon reached an early peak, with queues forming outside the *Strand Magazine* offices in London on the monthly publication days. In America alone, the print run of the magazine was increased by nearly 200,000 copies.

WALTER PAGET AND SIDNEY PAGET *(left, above). Although Walter had been the intended illustrator for the* Strand *stories, the project was mistakenly sent to Sidney, who then modelled his illustrations of Holmes on his younger brother.*

REICHENBACH FALLS *(right)*. *A late-Victorian colour print of the famous Swiss waterfall where Moriarty and Holmes had their final bout.*

LETTER TO DOYLE *(far right)*, *1904, from a reader offering a housekeeper to assist the retired Sherlock Holmes.*

ARTHUR WONTNER AND LYN HARDING *portraying Holmes and Moriarty in the 1935 British film* The Triumph of Sherlock Holmes.

The Return from Reichenbach

In 1903, the event which all Holmesians had hoped for occurred, when Doyle was offered the then record sum of $45,000 by *Collier's* to produce thirteen new short Holmes stories. Sherlock Holmes rose from a watery grave, which was shown to have never existed, in *The Empty House*. These stories were later collected as *The Return of Sherlock Holmes*, but many enthusiasts considered that the resurrected Holmes was never as good as he had been. (This was, perhaps, an early example of something familiar to modern followers of long-running television programmes – the "third-series syndrome", where the plots become more mechanical and repetitive and the characters lack fresh development!) The collection does, however, contain some great stories.

A further series of adventures began their individual publication in 1908 with *Wisteria Lodge*. This collection of eight stories, known as *His Last Bow*, did not appear until 1917, with the last of the four Holmes long stories, *The Valley of Fear*, intervening in 1914–15. The collection included *The Cardboard Box*, an older story which Doyle had suppressed from his collected publication at the time of *The Memoirs*. The final collection of Holmes short stories, which began individual publication in 1921, was issued as *The Case-Book of Sherlock Holmes* in 1927, and many of these stories are definitely considered to be of inferior quality. The last story to be written was *Shoscombe Old Place*, although chronologically it takes place before Holmes's final adventure, which is *His Last Bow*.

The Sherlock Holmes Phenomenon

With the death of Sir Arthur Conan Doyle in 1930 the full range of Sherlock Holmes narratives was four long stories and 56 short stories: these stories have become known as the Sherlock Holmes Canon, or more simply as the 'Canon'. There are some additional pieces by Doyle which contain Holmes as a character, such as a very short story written to be produced as a miniature book for the royal doll's house at Windsor, and some references to an amateur consulting detective in other Doylean stories, such as *The Man with the Watches* and *The Lost Special*, but the world's continuing demand for Holmes stories has otherwise had to be met, with enormously varying degrees of success, by the many authors who have since produced pastiches and parodies about the "Master" and adaptations of the original stories.

Public demand for Holmesian adventures has also been met by the worlds of theatre, film and television. Perhaps the most popular stage actor to portray Holmes was William Gillette, whose 1899 play *Sherlock Holmes* was a massive success in America and, later, in England. This play introduced

THE SAINTSBURY PIPE (above). This specially sculpted pipe, a portrait of the actor H.A. Saintsbury, was presented to him by his producer, Charles Frohman, on the occasion of Saintsbury's 500th performance as Sherlock Holmes on 21st December, 1903.

WILLIAM GILLETTE AS HOLMES *(left above) surrounded by some of the other characters represented in the Canon.*

SHERLOCK HOLMES STARRING WILLIAM GILLETTE *(left and below) from the 1916 film based on his long running play. In the scene of the arrest of Moriarty, Gillette is pictured second from the right. Below, the actress Marjorie Kay portrays Alice Faulkner, Holmes's erstwhile love interest in the stage version. Gillette based Alice Faulkner on Irene Adler from* A Scandal in Bohemia.

WILLIAM GILLETTE (*above*) *as he appeared in his stage play* Sherlock Holmes, 1900. *Gillette was famous for his portrayal of the great detective on both sides of the Atlantic.*

EILLE NORWOOD (*right above*) *in the play* The Return of Sherlock Holmes, 1923. *He was best known for his screen appearances as the master sleuth, portraying Holmes in 47 silent films.*

BASIL RATHBONE *became Hollywood's most famous Holmes, yet the 1953 version of the play* Sherlock Holmes *(below) by Ouida Rathbone, the actor's wife, lasted for only three performances. His earlier portrayals of the detective, as in* The Adventures of Sherlock Holmes *(right), with Nigel Bruce as Watson, 1939, were more enduring.*

the public to one of the most famous Holmesian accoutrements, the curved pipe, an object not specifically mentioned in the stories, which Gillette used primarily because he could not speak his lines with a straight pipe in his mouth.

More films have been made about Sherlock Holmes than about any other character in the literature of the whole world, with one actor, Eille Norwood, appearing in 47 different Holmes films. Arthur Wontner gave an interesting interpretation of Holmes in the thirties, although many considered him to be too old for the part. In the forties, Basil Rathbone rapidly became identified as the archetypal screen Holmes of his time, although few of the scripts of his fourteen Holmes films had any connection with the Doylean Canon. Unfortunately, Rathbone's Watson, Nigel Bruce, was forced to play his part as a bumbling fool, which did a great and lasting disservice to the more intelligent and subtle original.

More accurate film renditions of Watson have since appeared, with André Morell in *The Hound of the Baskervilles* and with James Mason's particularly sympathetic version alongside Christopher Plummer's Holmes in the non-Canonical *Murder by Decree*.

Television has been a singularly effective medium for Holmes. Louis Hector was in fact the first TV Holmes, in a field test broadcasting of *The Three Garridebs* which appeared months before the official commencement of TV services in the USA, in 1937. Douglas Wilmer and Peter Cushing starred in important Holmesian series for British television in the late sixties, which better revealed the potential for Holmes on the small screen. In the late eighties and early nineties, Granada TV in Britain devoted a great deal of research and resources to producing what has certainly been seen as the definitive Holmesian series of the period, with Jeremy Brett providing a finely studied if occasionally over-mannered representation of Holmes. Much of the success of the series has come from the excellent performances of David Burke and, latterly, of Edward Hardwicke as Watson, for the importance of this character is often under-emphasized in the visual adaptations of the Canon, where Watson's fine descriptive powers are no longer an essential requirement.

The Future

The centenary of the first Holmes story, in 1987, saw celebrations around the world, and a massive increase in interest in all matters connected with Holmes. It seems that this interest will continue to grow as each generation finds something new to meet their own requirements in that Holmesian world which is ever the same, yet always new.

MICHAEL CAINE *(below) as an unconventional, bumbling Holmes in a publicity still from the film* Without A Clue.

JAPANESE PROGRAMME FOR *SHERLOCK'S LAST CASE (left). Charles Marowitz's play appeared in Japan in September 1988. The appeal of Baker Street is international and in Japan Holmes has one of the largest popular followings anywhere in the world.*

JEREMY BRETT *(far left) portrayed the detective in Granada Television's production of* The Hound of the Baskervilles, *as well as the successful series.*

SHERLOCK HOLMES AND HIS TIMES

The Holmesian Era

"Good old Watson! You are the one fixed point in a changing age." These words are part of Holmes's last speech in his final case, *His Last Bow*, and they show that Holmes was very much aware of the many changes which had occurred during his active life as a detective, which was in turn a reflection of the social awareness of his creator, Doyle. The unique nature of Holmes is revealed not only by the fact that he was born five years before his creator, in 1854, but by the supposition that he is still "alive" in 1992, sixty-two years after the death of his literary parent. Holmes's life has therefore spanned six reigns, two world wars and an almost total social revolution in the country of his birth. In considering Holmes in his most famous role, however, we must confine ourselves primarily to those years when he was active as a consulting detective. His first case was The *"Gloria Scott"* in 1873, and although he retired in late 1903 or early 1904, after *The Creeping Man*, he returned to serve his country prior to the outbreak of the First World War in *His Last Bow*; in all, a span of some 40 years during which Britain underwent considerable change.

Holmes's Education

Holmes describes himself as being the descendant of country squires and a grandson of a sister of the French artist Vernet (*The Greek Interpreter*). It is not recorded where he was born, although many supporters favour North Yorkshire, partly because of a house called "Mycroft" located on the moors. This author considers Derbyshire to be a strong contender, because of the presence of a branch of the Holmes family living in the vicinity of the Duke of Holdernesse, and because of Sherlock's very personally antagonistic attitude to that Duke during his visit to the Peak District in *The Priory School*.

Any form of education, beyond the most elementary, had to be paid for at that time,

OTTO LAGONI, *starring in a very loose interpretation of the detective of Baker Street in* The Confidence Trick, *a Danish film of 1910.*

PETER CUSHING (*opposite*) *as Holmes in a publicity still for the Hammer Films production of* The Hound of the Baskervilles, *1959.*

THE BOOKS AND JOURNALS IN HOLMES'S STUDY, *as featured in the Sherlock Holmes Pub in London. The pub has meticulously recreated the eclectic surroundings of the famous detective of 221B Baker Street.*

THE BOOKS AND JOURNALS IN HOLMES'S STUDY, *as featured in the Sherlock Holmes Pub in London. The pub has meticulously recreated the eclectic surroundings of the famous detective of 221B Baker Street.*

ledge which Watson describes so well in *A Study in Scarlet*. Sherlock must, however, have received a more than rudimentary education, since he did spend at least two years at a university (*The "Gloria Scott"*). Again, financial constraints, combined with Sherlock's natural propensities, may have resulted in his studying at one of the less socially prestigious universities, with Manchester being a likely contender in terms of curriculum and proximity to areas such as Derbyshire and Yorkshire, although the Canon does suggest that Holmes had at least some acquaintance with Oxford or Cambridge (see page 100).

either through a tutor or at preparatory and public schools (one should be aware that an English "public" school is in fact a private school, often involving boarding residence for pupils). Sherlock's elder brother, Mycroft, obviously received a sound, socially acceptable education, probably at one of the better public schools and then Oxford or Cambridge, for him subsequently to have become such an influential figure in the corridors of governmental power. There may have been some financial difficulties in providing a second son with a similar level of education, and this could perhaps help to explain Sherlock's lack of the sort of conformity which was bred at the public schools of that time, as well as the gaps in Sherlock's general know-

The Young Sleuth

Holmes was obviously not financially comfortable when he moved to London in 1874. Although the few cases which were brought to him by his college acquaintances helped him to pursue the specialist knowledge which he needed to become better able to deal with his later cases, he probably required some small assistance from his family to survive. When he first met Watson in 1881, he did so because he had informed Stamford that he needed someone to share the costs of the rooms which he had found at 221B Baker Street. Watson records that even in their earliest days together Holmes was visited by many peculiar characters, providing him with information or seeking

OLD BAKER STREET as it appeared when Holmes and Watson made their home and solved so many crimes there.

advice. Amongst the latter was Inspector Lestrade of Scotland Yard, and we must examine later Holmes's relationships with the official police.

In class-ridden Victorian society, Holmes appears to have been at ease with every level of that society, and he was not afraid to be openly critical of even the most highly-born of his clients, as with the King of Bohemia (*A Scandal in Bohemia*). There are suggestions of a resentment of social privilege in Holmes's attitudes, and this has even been taken to have been the product of some illicit relationship between a member of the nobility and a member of the Holmes family, a far from uncommon occurrence in British society at that time. A very explicit example of this is recorded in connection with John Clay in *The Red-Headed League*.

Holmes's often-mentioned drug abuse occurs primarily in the early part of his career, although there are indications that the temptations continue later, but this would have been seen as a less serious problem than it is now. Many strong drugs were then in common use, with laudanum, an alcoholic tincture of opium, still being available for quietening fractious infants. Many respectable physicians were regularly

experimenting with drugs which are now realized to be potentially very dangerous, with Doyle carrying out such experiments on himself at one stage in his career.

As Holmes became busier, the time available for his study of the new technologies for investigation of crime decreased, and the "missing three years" following the Reichenbach incident in 1891 must have provided an excellent opportunity for Holmes to progress with researches such as those he carried out on coal-tar derivatives in Montpellier (*The Empty House*). He also broadened his understanding of many other aspects of the world and its ways, whilst visiting such almost inaccessible rulers as the Dalai Lama in Tibet and the Khalifa at Khartoum. His report to the Foreign Office on the latter visit must have established his potential for useful work in a later age, in more complicated international negotiations. The contacts Holmes must have made during his residence in France in that period may also have been helpful between the two wars, especially in the early 1920s when diplomatic differences arose between England and France.

Holmes's Later Career

Holmes's many successes, and the publicity given to them by Watson, certainly served a most useful function for Holmes in bringing him even more interesting cases. He appears to have had a general disinterest in monetary matters, although those cases

SCIENCE OF SLEUTHING (*above left*). The Radio Times, *in celebration of the centenary of* A Study in Scarlet, *published this article dedicated to the mastery and intrigue of Sherlock Holmes.*

BAKER STREET (*above*) *in the mid-1890s, looking towards Marylebone Road. The busy street scene is typical of what Holmes would have seen when he ventured out of 221B.*

CLUTTERED CORNER OF HOLMES'S STUDY (*left*) *complete with various walking sticks for many of the detective's disguises, and chemicals that were used, among other things, for forensic experiments when analyzing clues.*

INTERIOR VIEWS OF HOLMES'S STUDY. *The Sherlock Holmes Pub has painstakingly recreated the study of 221B Baker Street, including artefacts relevant to many of the cases in the Canon. Notice the picture of Irene Adler on the mantelpiece (above right) and the harpoon used on a pig in* The Adventure of Black Peter.

which did pay well must have left him very comfortably provided for, as is shown by the high rent which Watson says that Holmes paid over the years for his rooms in Baker Street (*The Dying Detective*). He was also able to pay a high price, through the agency of his distant relative, Doctor Verner, for Watson's Kensington practice when Watson moved back in with Holmes after his return from his post-Reichenbach travels (*The Norwood Builder*). Perhaps his greatest mark of success was his audience with "a certain gracious lady" in 1895, and her presentation to him of a remarkably fine emerald tie-pin (*The Bruce-Partington Plans*). It is significant that Holmes never received any official rewards for his services, particularly as his brother Mycroft had suggested that these were available, and this again indicates Holmes's indifference, or disdain even, for the formal recognitions of Victorian life.

It also appears strange that at the age of only 50, seemingly at the peak of his career, Holmes retired. More so than Watson, he perhaps realized that the world was rapidly changing, and the new world may have been less to his tastes. Like his literary creator, he may well have been disgusted with the nature of man and his politics, as revealed through the disasters, disgraces and sheer inhumanity of the Boer War. It may, however, have been an increasing sense of boredom with the lack of originality in the cases which were being brought to him, for there are only a limited number of possibilities for originality in crime, and Holmes must have experienced most of them. Indeed it needed a threat to the safety of his country to bring him fully out of retirement for his final case.

The tensions which had built up in Europe between Holmes's retirement in 1903–4 and his temporary return to service in 1914 are very apparent in the conclusion of *His Last Bow*. Holmes had spent the early part of his retirement on the South Downs, where he kept bees, read philosophy and began writing the definitive study of detection, although his peaceful way of life was disturbed by the arrival of crime at his own door in *The Lion's Mane*. He was to return to this quiet solitude during and after the First World War, but it does seem to be almost unthinkable that he has not become involved in the momentous events which have occurred since 1914. Perhaps, as Watson has been busy elsewhere, any exploits which have involved Holmes have not been so dramatically or publicly recorded.

In addition, the nature of the investigations carried out by Holmes have tended to reflect the times in which he has lived, and as any more recent cases involving Holmes may well have been more far-reaching in their consequences, Holmes may increasingly have had to emulate his elder brother by becoming the silent adviser of those who need his great abilities. Scotland Yard today uses a computer system known as HOLMES (Home Office Large Major Enquiry Service) to assist them in solving crimes. One cannot but help wonder whether this is merely a front, and that a certain unlisted telephone number in the South of England is actually very well known to a few of the descendants of Inspector Lestrade.

Holmes and "a Bad Lot"

Holmes inevitably interacted with the official force on many occasions, and they are generally shown to be inefficient if not actually incompetent in contrast with him. There had been numerous attempts at improving the policing of the nation, but a regularized force was not established until 1829, when the Metropolitan Police were introduced by Sir Robert Peel. It was from their founder's name that policemen were to be known as "Bobbies" and "Peelers". The headquarters of this force was at Scotland Yard in Westminster. A specialized

Detective Department was set up in 1842, with only two detectives, and this strength had risen to only fifteen by 1868. Corruption became rife in this department, and following the so-called "Trial of the Detectives" in 1877, the department was largely

"BOBBIES". *Fashion in Britain changed drastically from the Victorian era to the 1930s for all but the Metropolitan police. The policeman of 1934 (left) wore a uniform virtually identical to that of his Victorian predecessor (below). The latter has a Bull's-eye lantern on his belt.*

METROPOLITAN POLICE WAGON *from the late 19th century (below left). The wagons were used for mass arrests during large riots like those of "Bloody Sunday".*

SIR EDWARD BRADFORD
(below), *Commissioner of the
Metropolitan Police, during
the final years that Inspector
Lestrade worked with Holmes.*

[SCOTLAND-YARD, THE HEAD-QUARTERS OF THE METROPOLITAN POLICE.]

SCOTLAND YARD. *New
Scotland Yard (above) became
the headquarters of the
Metropolitan Police in 1890
after a terrorist bomb
damaged the original
building (above right).*

re-staffed and reorganized as the Criminal Investigation Department (CID) in 1878. Lestrade and Gregson, who were described as being "the pick of a bad lot" by Holmes in 1881, may have cleanly survived the 1877 trial, for Lestrade certainly remarked that he had more than twenty years' experience in *A Study in Scarlet*. In a terrorist bombing attack in 1884, the CID offices were almost destroyed, and the headquarters moved to new premises at New Scotland Yard on the Embankment in 1890.

The CID had no powers outside of the Metropolitan districts of London, but they could be requested to provide help by the chief constable of another force. This procedure does not appear to have been followed when Holmes invited Lestrade to travel down to Dartmoor to assist with the conclusion of the Baskerville murder case. Holmes was correct, however, when he mentioned that Lestrade had been retained by the friends of James McCarthy to work on the case in the latter's favour in *The Boscombe Valley Mystery*, since the 1839 Metropolitan Police Act did allow private groups and individuals to hire policemen, provided that the full costs were borne by such people. This may give an entirely new meaning to the Holmesian phrase "engage a special", but it may also explain how Holmes was able to call in Lestrade for the Baskerville case.

There was a general discontent with conditions in the police, and these did not begin to improve until a new commissioner was appointed in 1890. Sir Edward Bradford visited all of his stations and soon put right many of the grievances. He also introduced a newspaper, known as *The Police Gazette*, and although this was only intended for police forces it would have provided an excellent source of information for Holmes, who no doubt arranged to obtain regular copies through one of his police contacts.

The reforms at Scotland Yard also extended into the fields of scientific detection, and many of the methods of Sherlock Holmes became the basis for developments in forensic science. Holmes's careful observation and recording of the scene of a crime became a standard procedure with the CID, as did Doyle's suggested use of plaster casts of foot impressions. Holmes does make several references to finger and thumb marks in solving some of his cases, but the use of fingerprints as a means of uniquely identifying individuals was not adopted by Scotland Yard until 1901.

The 1880s saw a great deal of social unrest in Britain, much of it associated with an economic depression, but also with problems such as the unpopularity of the monarchy resulting from the Queen's withdrawal from public affairs after the death of her beloved Prince Albert. There was also an increase in sexually orientated crimes, and with this came an increasing popularization of discussions of the psychological causes of such problems, although some have claimed that the relationship may have been partially the other way around. Holmes himself made attempts to reconstruct crimes from the viewpoint of the criminal, and this too became a standard practice of detection. It is also significant that when Watson first meets Holmes, the latter has just developed an infallible means of chemically identifying blood stains. Once again this reflects not only Holmes's advanced procedures, but Doyle's own wide interests and his attempts at making both the public and officialdom aware of the potentials of new sciences and methodologies. Holmes was also aware of longer-term trends in crime, and he frequently quotes previous cases from his in-

"BLOODY SUNDAY" (above). The workers' riot of 1887 in London.

dexes where similar methods had been used before. This was an approach that was to be fully developed by the official force through the Criminal Records Office, with the result that the repeated use of a particular *modus operandi* by a criminal has often resulted in his or her downfall.

A general decrease in the crime rate during the 1890s allowed the establishment of better relationships between the police and the public, as well as time for the further development of improved methods of policing and crime detection. Although Holmes was generally disparaging about the police in his early career, he does suggest that in this later period they led the world in thoroughness and method (*The Three Garridebs*). One area in which there still appears to have been a problem was that of class. Lestrade is described as being an inspector in 1881, and he may have held that rank for some time by then. Although Holmes frequently points to Lestrade's ineptitude, it is Lestrade who is given the credit for solving many of Holmes's cases, as far as the authorities were concerned. In spite of this apparent success he is still an

BERTILLON INSTRUMENTS (right below) for measuring bone size. This was one standard method of criminal identification used by the Metropolitan police in the late-Victorian era.

"AN ARREST" (left below).

ORIGINAL HANDCUFFS AND TRUNCHEON (below) as used by the first "Bobbies".

inspector in 1895. Perhaps the relationship between Sherlock Holmes and the police can best be summarized in an alleged incident in the life of the creator. When Doyle arrived in Egypt in 1895 he supposedly found that the Sherlock Holmes stories had been translated into Arabic and issued to the local police as a textbook!

Holmes and Crime

The Victorian public was fascinated by sensational crime, and the press eagerly satisfied that fascination. Holmes himself is described by Watson as having an immense knowledge of sensational literature. There do seem to have been fashions in crime,

THE WHITECHAPEL HORRORS. *The most celebrated serial murder cases of late-Victorian London. The speculation over the true identity of the infamous Jack the Ripper continues to this day while the questions of cover-up grow. Yet perhaps the most intriguing question is why wasn't Sherlock Holmes consulted?*

probably as a result of imitations of some of the more lurid crimes given coverage by the newspapers. There was a great popularity in late-Victorian London for dismembering murder victims and distributing the parts around the city. One particularly audacious murderer travelled by omnibus, carrying the head of his victim wrapped in a napkin on his knees. It is probably apocryphal, however, that he almost gave himself away by paying double after asking the fare and being told that it was "sixpence a head"!

Much of the crime of the time was, however, less grotesque, although of a nature which was particularly abhorrent to the middle and upper classes of Victorian society, being crimes against property. As with many other aspects of Victorian morals, there was an ambivalence between the supposed public attitudes to crime and actual private, individual attitudes. At the end of the century Doyle's brother-in-law, E.W. Hornung, began to produce a series of stories about an upper-class gentleman-criminal called Raffles, a character who quickly caught the admiration of a wide audience. Holmes himself was not averse to committing such crimes as burglary in the pursuit of those he suspected, and he occasionally acted as his own court of law in deciding whether those he discovered to be criminally guilty should be brought before the official courts.

The question must, almost inevitably, be asked as to why Holmes does not appear to have been called in to assist the police with the most notorious crime of the age, the "Jack the Ripper" murders which occurred in 1888. It does seem unlikely that Holmes would not have involved himself in the investigation, even if he was not consulted officially, and it would seem equally unlikely that – being who he was – he would not have found the criminal, or criminals, involved. Thus it is possible that he did just this, and that there was no subsequent public recognition of the fact because of some political, high-society or simple police embarrassment involved in the solving of the notorious crime. It certainly seems strange that the hundreds of extra policemen drafted into the Whitechapel district were all suddenly withdrawn shortly after the last murder, when no culprit had been found. It is a fact that the Metropolitan

Police commissioner of that time deliberately interfered with some of the evidence, and that he was later forced to resign in the face of public allegations of incompetence. It is also true that the Scotland Yard documents relating to the crime were closed to public inspection for many decades, and that some of those documents are now missing. Perhaps those missing documents revealed not only the criminal but also that a certain consulting detective had been foremost in discovering his identity. (See page 45 for another possible view.)

Sherlock Holmes and Communications

Holmes's methodology required a constant availability of accurate and current information. Much of this he obtained from newspapers, which helped to maintain his own meticuously filed index system, although he did inform Watson that his reading of such periodicals was restricted to the crime reports and the agony columns. Holmes had a very wide choice of reading available to him, with sixteen different London newspapers being mentioned in the Canon in addition to the many provincial news sources. His belief that the ability to identify different newspapers from the typeface they used and the quality of materials was "one of the most elementary branches of knowledge to the special expert in crime" is stated in *The Hound of the Baskervilles*, and this was yet another area where the official police were to follow his lead.

MAGNETO WALL TELEPHONE *(above). When not sending telegraphs or posting letters the modern Magneto is certainly the method of urgent communication Holmes would have used in his later cases.*

HOLMES'S LOCAL LETTER BOX *(left). Removed in 1963, this letter box on Chiltern Street was the nearest to what would have been 221B Baker Street and the one most likely used by Holmes and Watson.*

EDWARDIAN SONG SHEET. *Despite the telephone's popularity in the early 1880s, it is doubtful that Holmes would have ever attempted the tune "Ring Up Britain" on his violin.*

would stop the messenger boys from making their deliveries (*The Six Napoleons*).

For even more rapid communications, however, Holmes's favourite medium was the telegram, as Watson attests when he remarks that Holmes had never been known to write where a telegram would serve (*The Devil's Foot*). The first public telegraph system had been opened in 1843, covering the twenty miles between Paddington and Slough, and within two years its potential for police work was revealed when a suspected murderer, John Tawell, was arrested at Paddington after a message had been passed from Slough when the suspect boarded a train there. As the telegraph system did not include the letter "Q" in its alphabet, Tawell was described as being "in the garb of a Kwaker", and this rendition of Quaker was sufficiently understood for him to be identified. The telegram did have the obvious disadvantage of needing a telegraph office for the message to be sent, as this could often be at many miles' distance from a particular location, as with the Grimpen Post Office for Baskerville Hall, but it was almost worth having the telegraph invented to allow Holmes the imperiousness with which he summoned Watson by telegram with "Come at once if convenient – if inconvenient come all the same. S.H." (*The Creeping Man*).

For once Scotland Yard does seem to have been in advance of Holmes in the employment of one of the most convenient forms of communication, the telephone. Inspector Athelney Jones suggested telephoning the Yard in 1888 (*The Sign of Four*), whereas the first reference to a telephone at 221B Baker Street occurs ten years later (*The Retired Colourman*). The telephone certainly must have become essential for contacting Holmes once he retired to his house on the South Downs.

How Holmes Travelled

Holmes's journeys around London are almost inevitably associated with the hansom cab. These two-wheelers were a rapid and exhilarating form of transport, but one that was also noisy, uncomfortable and constantly in danger of overturning. Holmes does use many other forms of carriage, with

Holmes also transmitted and received information by letter, and here he had a far better national service than is now available, with up to a dozen deliveries of mail each day. It was commonplace in London to post a letter in the morning and receive the reply in the afternoon of the same day, and even on Dartmoor the letters which Watson sent to Baker Street were delayed by only a day before reaching Holmes back on Dartmoor. In addition to this, a more direct mail and parcel delivery service was possible through agencies such as the district messenger services, albeit at twice the Post Office rates. Holmes thoroughly trusted the reliability of such services, remarking that only murder

HOLMES AND WATSON
HAILING A HANSOM CAB.
A Paget illustration for
The Adventure of the
Cardboard Box.

the four-wheeler brougham being far more conducive to a safe and comfortable journey. It should be noted that when Watson (*The Dying Detective*) and Holmes (*The Final Problem*) whistle for a cab, they are not engaged in any vulgar practices involving the fingers being placed in the mouth, as Victorian gentlemen usually carried a special high-pitched cab whistle, with one blast summoning a four-wheeler and two a hansom. A cab journey across London would have been at around the same speed as today, as the traffic was almost as heavy, although the streets were far dirtier, with the deposits from the horses often only being removable at night. It is only in 1914, in Holmes's final recorded case (*His Last Bow*) that the motor car intrudes on the scene. Perhaps it is relevant that the then 62-year-old man about town, Watson, has learned to drive, whereas Holmes more fittingly remains part of the horse-drawn age for short journeys.

The underground railway did provide a more rapid method of transit in London, with the first line, the Metropolitan Railway, opening in 1863 to provide a three-and-a-half mile journey from Baker Street. In its first year this line carried over nine million passengers, which demonstrates the already-crowded nature of the city and its transport systems. This line, typical of the early lines, was very dirty, as the trains were steam-hauled. The first electric underground railway line did not open until 1896.

Holmes's journeys to the provinces and beyond were made primarily by railway, and he once again had a far better service available to him in many ways. Prior to 1923, Britain's railways were owned by hundreds of independent companies, and most of these were small branch-line companies feeding passengers to the main-line company routes all over the country. Competition between main-line companies often

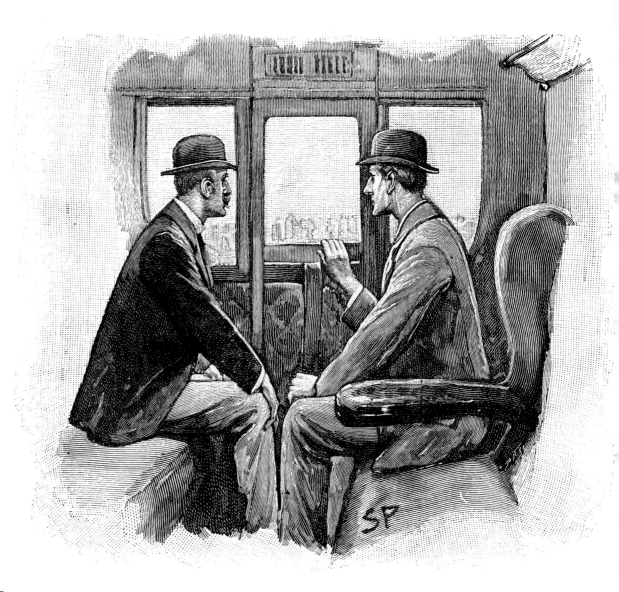

TRAVELLING BY RAIL. *Holmes and Watson take in the "sordid" view of London from their compartment. A Paget illustration for* The Naval Treaty.

resulted in journey times which were not much slower than today. On-board facilities were sometimes luxurious, although not always so, and Holmes's Inverness cape may often have been used for its proper purpose, with the shoulder cape being pulled over the head for warmth on some long, draughty journeys.

The intricacies of the railway connections needed on rail journeys would have required some dexterous use of that indispensable item for the rail traveller, *Bradshaw's Railway Guide*, which was published monthly in Victorian times. Even within one company's lines, frequent changes would often have to be made. Holmes's casual suggestion on Canterbury station that he and Watson would change their destination from Dover to Newhaven would actually have involved at least three changes of train on the London, Brighton and South Coast Railway Company's lines and

would have taken at least six hours to complete. Holmes's statement that they would reach Brussels that night, after leaving Canterbury at lunch-time, was a little optimistic.

Holmes obviously used sea ferries for his various trips to the Continent, and on his wider world travels to Tibet and America, but the only sea journey which he mentions specifically is that in *The Final Problem*, from Newhaven to Dieppe. Faster ships had been introduced on this route in 1875, with a golden guinea being placed by the ship's captain on the top of the engine room hatch of the *Paris II* for the fireman if the crossing was made in under five hours, though this timing was not achieved until 1888. However, by the time that Holmes made his crossing the record had been reduced to under three and a half hours – which compares well with the four hours taken today. Holmes will have been concentrating on other problems during the crossing, but

BULL'S-EYE LANTERN. *Referred to as a "dark lantern" in* Speckled Band, Red-Headed League, Bruce-Partington Plans, Charles Augustus Milverton, Six Napoleons, *and* The Sign of Four, *this early flashlight (below) was often used by Holmes when forced to search for clues or suspects at night. In an untypically authentic way Basil Rathbone (left), as Hollywood's Sherlock Holmes, illuminates the scene with a Bull's-eye lantern.*

Watson may have recalled an accident which had occurred on that route only four years previously, when the *Victoria* went aground in fog and was subsequently lost. Nineteen passengers were drowned when a lady's wrap caught in the ropes and up-turned the lifeboat in which they were being lowered. The macabre nature of the accident was increased when the cargo of black crepe slowly floated out from the hold to cover the ship in a dark shroud. Although many see the late-Victorian period as a golden age for travel, it was clearly not without its perils.

THE WORLD OF SHERLOCK HOLMES

HOLMESIAN AND SHERLOCKIAN SOCIETIES

Holmesians and Sherlockians

Holmesians and Sherlockians are those who, to varying degrees, are involved in Canonical scholarship, the study of the Sherlock Holmes stories. One must, naturally, ask what the difference is between Holmesians and Sherlockians, and the best answer is probably that of the American scholar who suggested that British Sherlockians prefer to call themselves Holmesians, whereas American Holmesians prefer to be called Sherlockians. This difference is probably a reflection of national character, with the British being more formal in their use of surnames and the Americans demonstrating their general affability with the use of forenames. The British practice is Canonically more correct, since Victorian gentlemen would almost invariably use surnames between themselves, other than when addressing relatives. Only Mycroft ever calls Holmes "Sherlock", although Mr Sherman does rather impudently refer to Holmes as "Mr Sherlock" in *The Sign of Four*. Even Watson, always calls him Holmes, and, being British, this author chooses to follow the practice of that greater writer. Scholarly activities associated with Holmes are not, however, limited to these two nations, as there are followers of Holmes in almost every country of the world.

Sherlock Holmes Societies

The senior Sherlock Holmes society of the world is generally recognized as being "The Baker Street Irregulars" of the USA. This society was founded in 1934, and although it has a deliberately small membership, it does have hundreds of affiliated scion societies throughout the USA. The names of some of these scion societies are an entertainment in themselves, with "The Afghanistan Perceivers", "The Bruce-Partington Planners", "The Giant Rats of Sumatra", "The Inverness Capers" and "The Scion of the Four" to mention only a

THE SHERLOCK HOLMES PUB *(above). An atmospheric view of the interior.*

SHERLOCK HOLMES PUB *(left). The sign, based on a Paget illustration, outside the pub near Charing Cross and Trafalgar Square. The pub is full of Holmesian memorabilia, including a finely reconstructed sitting room of 221B Baker Street. The pub is also of interest to Holmesian scholars because it used to be known as The Northumberland Hotel, which is where Sir Henry stayed when he first arrived in London (see* The Hound of the Baskervilles*).*

BASIL RATHBONE *as Sherlock Holmes, with briar pipe (opposite). A publicity still from the 1939 film* Adventures of Sherlock Holmes.

SHERLOCK HOLMES PUB. *The exterior of the pub (above right) is reproduced in a ceramic model (above).*

few. With some scholars claiming up to five wives for Watson, and with the repeated calls upon his time by Holmes, it is rather charming that there is also a scion society dedicated to the memory of "Doctor Watson's Neglected Patients". It is perhaps a little more surprising that there is a scion society called "The Brothers Three of Moriarty", although their true feelings are perhaps revealed by the fact that they hold an "Unhappy Birthday You Bastard Moriarty Celebration" each year, where buffalo droppings are added to a memorial pile!

In Britain the main society is "The Sherlock Holmes Society of London", which was

founded in 1951. One of the best-known activities of this society is their occasional re-creation of the famous fight between Holmes and Moriarty at the Reichenbach Falls in Switzerland, with over a hundred members in full Victorian costume present, each representing a character from the Canon. This large society does not have scion societies, but there are several independent regional Holmesian societies throughout Britain, ranging from "The Fratton Lodgers" in Holmes's literary birthplace of Portsmouth in the South to "The Northern Musgraves" in the North. A full

221B 1951 EXHIBITION. *The room was reconstructed for the Festival of Britain. It was in fact this exhibition which brought together many of the founders of what is today the Sherlock Holmes Society of London.*

register of independent British societies is maintained by "SHERLOCK" (Sherlock Holmes Enthusiasts Regionally Located Outside the Capital of the Kingdom).

Another major society in the world is "The Japan Sherlock Holmes Club", who were responsible for erecting the first life-size statue of Holmes. There are also smaller Japanese groups, such as "The Men with the Twisted Konjo"! Members of this society have paid homage to the Master at the Reichenbach Falls in traditional Samurai warrior costume, revealing the amazingly international appeal of Sherlock Holmes.

The above societies do accept members from other countries, but one truly international society is "The Franco-Midland Hardware Company", which is named after a fraudulent company set up in *The Stock-Broker's Clerk*, and which has its head office in England. This society provides a continuing correspondence study course on Sherlock Holmes, particularly aimed at those who are unable to attend the meetings of other societies, although it does also arrange its own meetings.

All of these societies, and those in other countries such as Australia, Canada, France, Germany and Spain are involved in similar activities: holding meetings with special lectures, discussions, quizzes and other amusements; publishing journals containing learned articles; and arranging expeditions to locations with Holmesian connections. Addresses are given on page 140 for contacting the main societies.

THE SITTING ROOM AT 221B *(above and left), a 1968 reconstruction by Adrian Conan Doyle at his Swiss château.*

BASIL RATHBONE · NIGEL BRUCE

SHERLOCK HOLMES *gefährlichster* AUFTRAG

GERMAN FILM POSTER *for the Hollywood film* Terror By Night.

THE CASE OF THE SHERLOCK HOLMES SCHOLARS

"The Game"

In many of their activities, the members of the Holmesian societies are involved in what may be called "The Game", although some members would insist that their involvement was purely academic and serious in terms of literary and historical studies. In playing The Game, one has to accept the premise that Sherlock Holmes was, and still is, a real person, and that Doctor Watson is his real biographer. Sir Arthur Conan Doyle is relegated to the mere role of the "Literary Agent" for Watson, although all Holmesians do, of course, have a great respect and admiration for him outside of The Game.

Having accepted these premises, attempts are then made to examine every aspect of the Canon in terms of actual historical events and locations. This can to a large extent be done, because the stories were recorded with an excellent eye for the social history of the time and for real locations, although of course a great deal of licence is attributable to the Literary Agent in those recordings. One major consequence of this process is that a large number of problems are thereby revealed within the Canon. The true explanation of many of these problems is that the Literary Agent was not always scrupulous with such literary disciplines as continuity control, and that he often concentrated several separate locations into one small region to improve the dramatic quality of the story. This explanation cannot, however, be accepted when playing The Game. Dedicated Holmesians also do not accept other, too-easy explanations, such as constantly attributing problems to Watson's notoriously bad memory, or to his habit of changing the facts to protect the innocent. A more interesting and challenging object for scholars is to explain the problems using only actual historical facts, the information contained in the Canon and good, logical arguments.

HOLMES AND MORIARTY *(above); the statuette of Moriarty is modelled on the Paget illustration for* The Final Problem.

THE GREAT DETECTIVE *(left), a ballet given by the Sadler's Wells Company in 1953, with Kenneth MacMillan as Holmes and Stanley Holden as Watson.*

HOLMES AND WATSON ON THE TRAIL OF THE HOUND *(opposite). Peter Cushing, right, and Andre Morell, left, in the 1959 Hammer Films production* The Hound of the Baskervilles.

"IT IS QUITE A THREE PIPE PROBLEM" (above). Holmes is never described as specifically smoking a calabash in the Conan Doyle stories; however, he is usually portrayed puffing on one in film and on stage, as Michael Caine (middle, in Without A Clue, *1989) and John Neville (right, in* A Study in Terror, *1965) demonstrate.*

Some Problems in the Canon

One might begin at the beginning by attempting to determine when Sherlock Holmes was born. No date is given in the Canon, but in *His Last Bow*, which takes place in August 1914, he is described as being a man of 60. This may have been a generalization, but the birth year of 1854 does fit well with other indications in the Canon, and is generally accepted by scholars. The birth day is even less clearly indicated, but the date of 6th January is again generally accepted – partly on the grounds of Holmes's fondness for quoting from Shakespeare's *Twelth Night* (or misquoting, as he does twice), and partly from indications in one case that a party may have taken place on the night before 7th January. Astrological analysis of Holmes's character, however, suggests that he is a Scorpio, with a birthday in November. It should perhaps be noted that the January date does allow Holmesians to celebrate his birthday in conjunction with New Year festivities!

It has been suggested that Holmes is still alive, which, in 1992, makes him 138 years old. This is possible because, the theory goes, following his escape from Reichenbach, Holmes travelled to Tibet, where he met the Dalai Lama and learned the secret of eternal life. He did finally retire in 1914, after *His Last Bow*, and he now lives on the South Downs, where he keeps bees, studies philosophy and is writing the definitive study on detection. He passed on the secret of eternal life to Watson, whose birth date has been calculated as being in 1852, ex-

VIGGO LARSEN LENDS AN EAR TO THE WOODWORK (below) as Holmes in a 1909 Danish film from Nordisk, Droske 519.

trapolated from the Canonical fact that he graduated from university in 1878.

Watson is supposed to be rather more actively engaged in his retirement. In *The Sign of Four*, Watson boasted that he had "an experience of women which extends over many nations and three separate continents", and he is currently travelling the remaining continents of the world to extend that knowledge further.

Holmes's early history is continued with considerations of which university he attended, with the primary contenders being Oxford and Cambridge. As with many other problems, the Canon itself provides only a few direct clues, and the remainder must be obtained from indirect evidence. In *The "Gloria Scott"*, Holmes mentions that he was at college for two years, and that he was bitten by the dog of a fellow student when on his way to chapel. Since college regulations in the 1870s banned dogs from the premises, it can be claimed that Holmes must have been bitten outside the college on his way into chapel. As Oxford students were in those days required to spend their first two years living in college, Holmes must have been at Cambridge, where students began with lodgings in the town. In *The Three Students*, however, Holmes refers to a quadrangle in a college, but quadrangles are known as courtyards at Cambridge, which suggests that he was an Oxford man. This is also suggested by his unfamiliarity with the Cambridgeshire countryside, and by his references to Cambridge as an inhospitable place, in *The Missing Three-Quarter*. Even the drawings of Sidney Paget are brought into the argument, when it is claimed that the hat band on Holmes's boater in *The "Gloria Scott"*, although drawn in black and white, appears to be light (blue), rather than dark (blue), thereby indicating Cambridge.

In 1988, The Sherlock Holmes Society of London spent their annual weekend expedition at Oxford proving conclusively that Holmes was an Oxford man. In 1989, the same society spent their annual expedition weekend in Cambridge, proving equally conclusively that he was a Cambridge man. The obvious conclusion from this might be that he attended both universities. Holmes's reference to spending two years at college would imply that he did not obtain a

HOLMES BRINGS HIS DEDUCTIVE SKILLS TO BEAR ON A HAT *in the 1965 film* A Study in Terror. *Billed as the "original caped crusader" in America, the dynamic duo of John Neville, as Holmes, and Donald Houston, as Watson, track down the notorious Jack the Ripper.*

degree, and this would agree with his habit of concentrating only on those elements of any subject which were of immediate use to him. This deliberation has not prevented other scholars from proposing Manchester or London universities as Holmes's alma mater, precisely because the subjects available at those universities would have been of more relevance to him. One scholar has even used evidence from the Canon to argue that Holmes must have attended Portsmouth Polytechnic, in spite of the fact that this institute was not founded until the 1960s. It should from this example alone be appreciated that Holmesian scholars do derive a great deal of fun, as well as more serious involvement, from their pastime.

Moving to an examination of Watson, it may be considered strange that a medical

A CAREFULLY BALANCED
BLEND OF 221B PIPE TOBACCO
MIXTURE *(below). Perhaps it
is the same blend of shag
tobacco Holmes enjoyed whilst
solving the case of* The Man
with the Twisted Lip?

man should suffer from the particular problem associated with him. On the very first page of the first Sherlock Holmes story, *A Study in Scarlet*, Doctor Watson informs us that he was wounded in the shoulder by a Jezail bullet at the Battle of Maiwand. Only a few years later, in *The Sign of Four*, he comments that he was wounded by a Jezail bullet in the leg. Investigations of "Watson's Wandering Wound" could fill several volumes of this size, but perhaps the best explanation is that his original, major wound was in the shoulder, and he was then wounded again, in the leg, as he was being evacuated from the battlefield. The varying intensity of the discomfort caused by these wounds would account for his different emphasis at different times. There are, however, still adherents of single-wound theories, who sometimes have to place the good doctor in some rather contorted positions to allow one bullet to wound both his shoulder and leg.

Medical considerations continue with an investigation of Holmes's drug abuse. Watson most graphically describes Holmes injecting himself with a seven-per-cent solution of cocaine in *The Sign of Four*, and there are other references to the use of morphine. Such references to drug abuse are primarily made in connection with Holmes's early career, and he explains his abuse on grounds of boredom with ordinary life. Watson later claims that he weaned Holmes off the habit, but it is much more likely that Holmes would simply have given up the habit when he became better known and thus received more interesting cases to deal with.

To return to Watson, there is a problem connected with his name. This is very clearly given by him as being John H. Watson, but nowhere in the Canon is it revealed what the "H" stands for. A problem connected with his first name occurs in *The Man with the Twisted Lip*, where his wife,

" 'DO YOU KNOW WHERE WE
ARE?' " *(far right), Holmes
asks Watson in* The Empty
House. *The two were
standing in Camden House,
the "Empty House", which
stands opposite 221B Baker
Street, photographed here in
1904.*

A POSSIBLE HOME FOR
HOLMES? *(right), the house in
Baker Street, photographed by
Dr Gray Chandler Briggs in
1921, claimed to be 221B.*

Mary, refers to him as James. It has been suggested that Mary would have had a natural dislike for the name John, because of its association with John Sholto, and that she might therefore have adopted a pet name for her husband. Dorothy L. Sayers suggested that this pet name was James as an anglicized version of Watson's middle name, Hamish, although others have since claimed that this is an incorrect translation.

It was mentioned in the Preface that almost everyone knows the address of Sherlock Holmes, yet this address itself becomes a major scholarship problem. During the period when Holmes was occupying his rooms in Baker Street, the numbers in that street reached only a two-figure level, and there was thus no number 221. The length of Baker Street has since been twice increased, firstly with the addition of the length of York Place and secondly with the length of Upper Baker Street. The current number 221 was originally in the latter of these streets. There are numerous descriptive clues in the Canon, although some of these, such as the reference to a plane tree in the back yard, may no longer be relevant. There should be seventeen steps between the ground floor and the first floor,

although this would have applied to many of the houses in the street and may also have been changed with time. Many clues are obtained from the description of the empty house opposite 221, "Camden House", and there are indirect indications as to the location, such as the fact that it appears to have been worthwhile catching a cab from Baker Street station to 221. The Literary Agent himself was somewhat evasive about the location, having on one occasion mentioned that he could not recall ever having been in Baker Street, although on another occasion he suggested that 221 was on the corner of George Street and Baker Street. This last suggestion shows the unreliability of the Literary Agent, since a corner site does not fit many of the requirements of the Canon. A general consensus is that the location is on the west side of Baker Street, somewhere between George Street and Crawford Street. This author's own preference is for number 31 Baker Street, but the original Victorian building no longer exists at that site.

The number of problems referred to above is only a small selection. There is space only for a minimal coverage of the evidence available and the possible solutions. Full volumes have been written on some of these problems, and there are many more which have not yet even been started on by scholars. For all those who are interested in playing The Game, the game is still very much afoot.

221B BRICK *removed from the original Victorian building and then sold for charity by Abbey National bank, the current occupier of 221B Baker Street.*

SECTION OF A LONDON STREET MAP *(above right) dating from 1870. Baker Street is located lower left.*

CHRISTOPHER LEE AS HOLMES. *The actor appeared as Holmes in the 1962 West German production* Sherlock Holmes and the Deadly Necklace *(above left). Needless to say, the costume got the thumbs down before it ever reached the film set.*

A SCHOLARLY CASE STUDY

The Problem of Sherlock Holmes
and Jack the Ripper
P.L. Anness

Lastly, and most controversially, we come to the greatest mystery in Holmes's career – on the principle of the dog that didn't bark – which is his apparent lack of involvement in the case of Jack the Ripper: the brutal slaying of five (or six, depending on the theory espoused) prostitutes in the East End of London between August and November in 1888. At this time Holmes was at his prime, and although he had not yet established his huge popular reputation, his work was well known and highly regarded in forensic circles, and he had already become the first point of call for the officials of Scotland Yard when they found themselves at a loss. It seems impossible, on the face of it, that he would not have been consulted on a matter which had so obviously baffled the authorities and which became, for a time, an issue which looked likely to destroy the nation's trust and belief in its police force – almost to the point of public disorder and riot.

A number of theories have been put forward to cover this omission. The commonly accepted explanation is that Holmes was involved in the case, and indeed solved it, but that the perpetrator was so positioned in the community – perhaps even of royal blood – that the detective was begged and persuaded not to reveal his findings for the good of the country. A second view, along the same lines, is that Holmes caught the criminal, but decided, again perhaps for political reasons, to take the matter into his own hands, and executed the killer himself rather than depending on the official mechanism.

Unfortunately there is a further theory, which, though abhorred by right-thinking people (including the authors of this volume), is included herein for the purposes of academic completeness. This is the hypothesis that Holmes himself was Jack the Ripper.

A profile of the Ripper was developed by the police at the time: necessarily primitive in those pre-Freudian days when neither the psychological nor the scientific fields of criminal investigation had reached any degree of sophistication. Essentially they were looking for a man who was almost certainly not a doctor, but who had some medical training or knowledge; someone who could move at will through the lowest sections of the community without drawing attention to himself; someone who could come and go as he pleased, with no parents, wife or friend living at home with him to observe his movements, demeanour, and condition; perhaps someone who had a knowledge of police procedures, so that he could anticipate and make counter moves against them; and certainly a man who had an antipathy towards women, who had perhaps been slighted or damaged by one, or who imagined some threat against himself from a female.

It is regrettable that Holmes fits the bill so precisely. Although not specifically trained in medicine, he took courses at the University of London Medical School, and his knowledge of anatomy is confessed by Watson to be "accurate, but unsystematic". Stamford, perhaps indicating something more sinister than was realized at the time,

HOLMES'S SITTING ROOM AT 221B *(opposite) as reconstructed at Adrian Conan Doyle's Swiss château, the Château de Lucens.*

45

states that "he has amassed a lot of out-of-the-way knowledge which would astonish his professors". At the University he would have mixed with medical students, and had access (as he was allowed into the building without supervision) to equipment, tools, and, potentially, corpses. Remember, the evidence of Stamford is that he has seen Holmes experimenting on the "subjects" (donated bodies) in the dissecting room by beating them with a stick. He innocently accepts Holmes's explanation that he is investigating "how far bruises may be produced after death", but is this the truth? If it is, then it is not much more bizarre to suggest that the murders of the Whitechapel prostitutes may have been the grotesque scientific experiments of a diseased mind, unable any longer to differentiate between live and dead subjects.

Holmes's talent for disguise is well established. Due to the circumstances of the Ripper murders, no reliable descriptions were ever obtained. Those that were received were contradictory, implying that the murderer took some pains to change his appearance from time to time. Nothing would have been simpler for Holmes – often seen as a groom, a loafer, a seaman, and even a priest – to take on the guise of a person whose presence would have raised no comment in Whitechapel. There were even fantastic rumours at the time that the Ripper was a woman – and Holmes, as we know, could easily assume a female role.

Regarding his ability to come and go as he pleased, Holmes was, at this time, living alone at Baker Street, as Watson, having met Mary Morstan, was almost certainly living with his new wife. This is one of the most confusing aspects of the history. Watson had clearly become engaged following the *Sign of Four* case, which occured, we are told, "some years after" *A Study in Scarlet*, which we gather took place in March 1887. Yet in *A Scandal in Bohemia*, which is dated March 1888 (five months before the first Ripper killing), Watson states that "my marriage had drifted us away from each other" and that he was living away from Baker Street. This brings us to Watson's role in the affair. It was often suggested that the Ripper had a helper, but given our knowledge of the doctor's character we can hardly suspect him of any active role. On the other

hand somebody who lived so close to the man could not, realistically, have been totally absent of some suspicions, however mild or unformed. The confusion of the dates by Watson is consequently interpreted as an unconscious suppression of facts that may have implicated his friend. Regardless, it is very highly probable that Holmes was living alone at this time, and could therefore act unobserved. He had, in any case, the contacts in the East End, and the intelligence, to set up a sanctuary for himself there if he thought it advisable. Indeed, it has been pointed out that Holmes had only to inform the police that he was investigating the crimes, and he could have set himself up a temporary headquarters in the area and come and go as he pleased – he was uniquely above suspicion.

His knowledge of police procedure, and contempt for it, are legendary – he could easily have double-crossed Aberline, or any of the other officers on the case. Again, it has been suggested that his scorn for the authorities, and his almost obsessive desire to make them look foolish and show himself superior, may have been a key motivating factor in the crimes. His other characteristics – the sociopathic desire for instant gratification and fear of boredom; manic mood swings from frenetic activity to overwhelming lassitude; an obsessive fascination with crime and its processes; an intensely secretive nature, intermingled with an uncontrollable desire for publicity; a tendency towards drug-taking; and a superiority complex which on innumerable occasions allowed Holmes to place himself above the law as a determiner of justice – complement the picture of the typical serial-killer.

The principal motivating factor, and the last item in the police profile, was obviously a hatred of, or contempt for, women. Unfortunately Holmes again falls under suspicion. Although Watson normally – perhaps, once more, unconsciously protecting his friend – describes Holmes's misogyny as a simple lack of interest, it is not difficult, reading between the lines, to develop a more sinister interpretation. One wonders what was really said when Holmes is reported, on hearing of his friend's engagement: "I really cannot congratulate you . . . love is an emotional thing, and whatever is emotional is opposed to that true cold

THE ILLUSTRATED POLICE NEWS (opposite), 1888, brilliantly catered to the Victorian's insatiable appetite for murder, mutilation and all things morbid. What sort of mind could have committed such crimes? Did the murderer reside in Baker Street? Why wasn't Holmes contacted? It is interesting to note that, like "The Mysterious Monster of the East-End", the perpetrator of "The Whitehall Mystery" (lower strip) was never apprehended.

reason which I place above all things. I should never marry myself, lest I bias my judgement." More ominously, he is described by Watson in *A Scandal in Bohemia* in the following terms: "as a lover he would have placed himself in a false position. He never spoke of the softer passions, save with a gibe and a sneer."

The report by Watson entitled *A Scandal in Bohemia* is particularly important to the Holmes-as-Ripper theory. It has been noted that it dates from March 1888, shortly before the Ripper killings began, and that it opens with the barely veiled admission of

Holmes's mental hatred of women at the time. There is every probability that this hatred had been fostered by Watson's marriage and desertion. Without commenting on Holmes's sexuality, if we review the events of the previous two years in his life, we can see what a shock Watson's departure from Baker Street would have caused in an already sensitive mind. We know that Holmes was a lonely man (rationalizing loneliness by constant protestations of misanthropy and concentration on his all-important work), brought up effectively as an only child as his brother Mycroft was

CLIVE BROOK AS SHERLOCK HOLMES *in a publicity still. The celebrated actor who played the detective on two occasions, in* The Return of Sherlock Holmes, *1929, and* Sherlock Holmes, *1932, was better known for other roles.*

seven years his senior and too old for true sibling companionship. His isolation from his parents is confirmed by the fact that, in all the thousands of words of Watson's reports, no mention is ever made of them. That his isolation is caused by the difficulties of his personality is affirmed by the reluctance of Stamford to encourage Watson to share lodgings with Holmes: "You mustn't blame me if you don't get on with him . . . You proposed this arrangement, so you must not hold me responsible." That Watson is nervous is also an undisputed fact: "It seems to me, Stamford . . . that you have some reason for washing your hands of this matter."

Having overcome all the normally insurmountable hurdles he encounters when formulating relationships, and settled down with Watson in what can only be described as a pseudo-marriage, it can readily be considered that this previously shunned and lonely person might very well have placed too high an emotional value on what the formidably heterosexual Watson naturally treated as a domestic arrangement of convenience. All the signs are there – showing off; playing hard to get; alternative moods of self-aggrandizement and feigned stupidity – to suggest that Holmes went through a courtship ritual with Watson, which went unnoticed by the simple focus of his attentions. Then comes the unexpected blow of the engagement. Watson, in Holmes's mind, is announcing that he is to divorce him, and marry, of all things, a woman.

The Adler case (*A Scandal in Bohemia*) could therefore not have come at a worse time from Holmes's psychological point of view. Perhaps on the way to recovery from being cut out of his friend's life and having his "marriage" destroyed by one woman, he is now bested and outwitted by another. This surely, if one is ever to espouse the Holmes-as-Ripper thesis, is the critical point, as it is easy to see how between March and August of 1888 Holmes's mind might further have deteriorated so that a few months later he was ready to start killing symbolic representations of the women who had disrupted both his personal and business life. That prostitutes should have been chosen is no surprise: they represented the antithesis of the purity of Mary Morstan;

the logical extension and the embodiment of Irene Adler's career as courtesan; and the dark side of the femininity in his own nature.

It is well known that in most instances of serial killing that remain unsolved, the murders come to a halt because the killer, coming to a realization of what he is doing, commits suicide. Indeed, this is the reason given in the Ripper case for strong suspicion against Montague Druitt. Holmes, as ever, must be considered too remarkable a man for such a simple resolution. The most likely theory is that he "caught himself", when investigating the case, and came to terms with what he had done. After a period of self-analysis, completed in 1891 by his faked disappearance from the world while he travelled, among other places, to Tibet, his rehabilitation was complete, and he then made amends by devoting the rest of his life to good.

Others have, of course, gone further. There is a theory that Holmes did not mend his ways, but stopped the serial killing because he feared capture. Then, having constructed the Reichenbach Falls mystery as an elaborate alibi, he slipped back into England to murder Mrs Watson, thereby regaining the affection of his lover, who rejoined him in Baker Street on his return. It is, indeed, strange that Holmes, freshly back from isolation in foreign parts, should appear to know so much about Mrs Watson's demise (see *The Empty House*, page 93). Others again have theorized that Professor Moriarty never existed, but was the black side of Holmes's own nature. The flight from Moriarty was Holmes's flight from his own black, murdering personality (the Ripper), and the struggle at the Falls was a Jungian symbol for Holmes's wrestling with all his darkest instincts in the wilderness. Having killed Moriarty (his desire to murder), he was free once more to re-enter society.

Whatever is believed about Holmes and the Ripper by others, the authors of this volume, though forced out of academic integrity to include these facts in order to present a well-rounded and comprehensive testament, nevertheless wish widely to distance themselves from such scurrilous speculation however well founded.

HOLMESIAN COLLECTABLES

Personal Collections and Investments

The enormous increase in the popularity of the Sherlock Holmes stories has been accompanied by a corresponding increase in the desire to collect any sort of items connected with Sherlock Holmes. These items vary greatly in quality and original price, but the limited quantities produced of some of the earlier items means that they are often now extremely valuable, and they have thus become investment items. Even some of the originally very cheap items are now greatly sought after by collectors. General production rates have recently become more attuned to the wider market for such items, but some pieces are still deliberately produced in limited numbers to increase their value after sale, and this is exactly what has happened. A general piece of advice is to buy everything of reasonable quality which one can afford, as it will

A UNIVERSAL FILM POSTER *(opposite) for one of the twelve Universal films that starred the Rathbone-Bruce partnership between 1942 and 1946.*

COMMEMORATIVE HOLMESIAN BADGES *(left) from around the world.*

EDWARDIAN COMIC POSTCARD *(far left) c.1910. Not one of Holmes's more famous cases.*

MINIATURE CHINA HEADS *(below) from left to right: Watson, Lestrade, Holmes, and Moriarty.*

Sherlock Holmes:— "Judging by the line of evidence there's a Lady in that house!"

A JAPANESE HOLMES (*above*). *Illustration by Kiyoshi Tanaka.*

FIRST EDITION The Hound of the Baskervilles, *1902 (above right).*

the subsequent owner. Dedications from one famous person to another, however, do increase the value of an item considerably. (It should be noted that all the prices given here are 1990 approximate values, with an exchange rate of two US dollars to the pound sterling.)

Manuscripts

Undoubtedly, the ultimate version of any of the stories in the Canon, in collectable terms, must be a Doylean manuscript. It should be noted here that the term "manuscript" means the original version of a story, whether that was handwritten or typewritten. The manuscript of *The Valley of Fear*, minus the epilogue, which appears to be lost for ever, was sold at auction in 1990 for over £150,000 ($300,000), including auction commission and tax! This exact manuscript was listed in *Scribner's Rare Book Catalogue* of 1943 at £550 ($1,100). Such items are rarely going to come onto the market, and their value is reasonably well known, so there is little chance of a bargain buy here. Although there is considerable interest amongst Holmesian scholars about the

almost certainly increase its value within only a few years, and one may regret having to pay the higher price later or not even being able to obtain the item.

A further general point is concerned with the dedication of Holmesian items, such as the signing of books and programmes by authors, actors, and so on. If the item is intended for a personal collection, then a personalized dedication obviously makes the item of greater value to the person included in the dedication. If the item is for investment purposes, then it is usually better to have a more general dedication, which might more easily be applicable to manuscripts, only three stories have so far been published as facsimile versions. These are *The Adventure of the Priory School*, *The Adventure of the Lion's Mane*, and *The Adventure of the Dying Detective*. The first of these is already a rather expensive collector's item.

The Canon

The variety of single and collected editions of the stories in the Canon is enormous, and many readers are surprised to find that the texts vary between different editions. Some of these editions are more valuable because of these variations, and others are important as milestones in the publishing history of the Canon. It is possible to form an interesting private collection of editions without including the more exotic and extravagant rarities.

Probably the most desirable single edition for any collector to dream about is an original 1887 edition of *Beeton's Christmas Annual*, containing the first publication of a Sherlock Holmes story. This was published in paper covers, and a copy in good condition is extremely rare. A copy was sold at auction in 1990 for over £30,000 ($60,000), a notable increase on the original price of one shilling (10 cents), and a good investment increase on the 1943 catalogue listing of £87 (£175)!

The first editions of the long stories and of the collections of short stories are essential items in any serious Holmesian collector's library, but these too are becoming prohibitive in price. A copy of *The Hound of*

the Baskervilles (1902) in good condition would cost around £800 ($1,600), but an interesting collection can be made with some of the less rare editions, costing under £20 ($40) in many cases, and with some of the later, cheaper reproductions.

THE LAST ADVENTURE OF SHERLOCK HOLMES. Illustrated cover for Collier's.

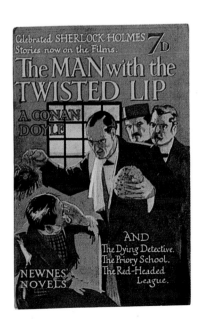

THE FIRST MOVIE TIE-INS *(left). Covers from the paperbacks for* The Resident Patient, The Man with the Twisted Lip, *and* The Empty House, *each starring Eille Norwood, 1921. Newnes published the tie-ins on the suggestion of Conan Doyle, but they were not a success.*

Pastiches, Parodies and Adaptations

A large number of Sherlock Holmes pastiches and parodies have been produced, most of them being of a very low standard, but some have become collector's items in their own right. A very popular series has been the *Solar Pons* stories by August Derleth, the original editions of which now fetch over £20 ($40) a copy, although newer paperback versions are now available. Others, such as Nicholas Meyer's *Seven-Per-Cent Solution*, are similarly more valuable in their first editions. Adaptations of the Canon, particularly in the form of scripts for television or radio, are extremely popular, with some author-signed adaptations being sold at over £100 ($200).

Magazines

Copies of the stories in the original *Strand Magazine* editions can be obtained for around £20–£50 ($40–$100), depending largely on condition, and everyone should perhaps attempt to find at least one of these to see how most of the stories were first seen. Complete sets are very rare items, and even a run of the nine *Strand*s containing *The Hound of the Baskervilles* can cost over £1,000 ($2,000). A less expensive way to obtain *Strand*s is in the six-monthly combined editions issued by the publishers in hardback covers, wherein one can often obtain six Sherlock Holmes short stories for around £30 ($60). The American equivalent of *The Strand Magazine* is *Collier's*, but copies of this magazine are often more difficult to find, even in America, and consequently more expensive.

Articles about Sherlock Holmes and Doyle are worth collecting from more general magazines, especially as their value is not often appreciated by those selling the

THE SIGN OF FOUR IN COMIC STRIP (far right) in issue 21, July 1944, from the American Classic Comics. *The edition also contains two non-Canonical stories.*

THE HOUND OF THE BASKERVILLES (below right) appeared in Classics Illustrated *issue 53, January 1947. The cover of the Greek edition (below far right) contains an interesting error: the missing red word, RACHE, is actually from* A Study in Scarlet.

THE NON-CANONICAL SHERLOCK STALKS THE JOKER (right) in The Joker Comic *number 6, April 1976. Holmes of the late twentieth century.*

magazines, but it can be hard work finding such items. In saving articles from current magazines, one should always save the whole magazine, rather than tear out the article, as complete magazines are not only more valuable but more interesting in placing the article in a historical context for later readers and collectors.

Another field for Holmesian interest is that of cartoon versions of the stories. There have been numerous issues of such items, but the value of these has risen very quickly, in line with the general increase in interest in the comic market. In 1990, some five-year-old £1 ($2) comics containing Sherlock Holmes were selling at around £20 ($40).

Film and Theatre Posters and Programmes

Some of the classic posters, such as an original Rathbone *The Hound of the Baskervilles*, now cost around £100 ($200), but there are reproductions available at £20 ($40), and some less expensive items can be obtained through film dealers, rather than

LOBBY CARD *(left) for the 1974 stage revival of* Sherlock Holmes. *An RSC production that first appeared at the Aldwych Theatre in London.*

CAMPAIGN BOOK *(above). The 1939 film was released as* The Adventures of Sherlock Holmes *in the U.S. and* Sherlock Holmes *in the U.K. A campaign book is supplied to the cinemas by the studios providing details of the story, the making of the film, publicity, and biographies of the actors.*

SPIDER WOMAN *(left), 1944, starring Basil Rathbone as Holmes and Gale Sondergaard as the eponymous villainess.*

Holmesian dealers. Foreign language versions of film posters can certainly make a collection more interesting. Programmes for some of the newer, major productions are now produced on a large scale, and these can often be obtained for less than £1 ($2), but some of the older programmes are very valuable. It is worth obtaining local

Photographs

production programmes, if only for the possibility that someone in the cast may later become more famous. (It is doubtful that anyone, apart from the lad's mother, originally bought a programme for the William Gillette play *Sherlock Holmes* because of the name of the young boy playing Wiggins, but Charles Chaplin's name certainly makes that a very collectable item today!) Again, with new productions, the value of a poster or programme can be increased by the autographs of the author or cast.

All pictures connected with Holmes are liable to become valuable, especially if they are signed. Even photographs of current Holmesian actors are selling for up to ten times their original price if they are signed, and loose photographs of some of the older stars are often very difficult to obtain. The market for such items has recently been more fully appreciated, with reproductions of many of the Rathbone publicity stills now becoming available at around £5 ($10).

BEN GREET COMPANY POSTER *1902.*

SHERLOCK HOLMES (above left). Poster for the first London production, 1901.

SHERLOCK HOLMES PROGRAMME *(above). An early revival of Gillette's play, this production is most notable for the fourteen-year-old actor who played Billy – Charles Chaplin.*

Games and Toys

There are usually several Holmesian games
commercially available at any particular
time, and these can quickly become collector's items once they go out of production,

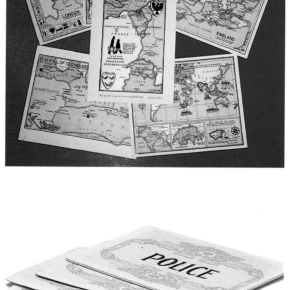

DONEGALL CHRISTMAS CARDS
*(right). Part of a series
designed by the American Dr
Julian Woolf for the eminent
Holmesian scholar Lord
Donegall.*

CARD GAME SET *(below),*
1904.

BOARD GAME *(far left), 1969.*

BAKER STREET HOTEL MUG

HOLMES EARTHENWARE BUST, *(near left) 1986.*

thereby increasing their value. Early versions of such games are now very much sought after. The value of games often depends on whether there are any original parts missing, such as various paper forms which may have been filled in when the game was played. Toys vary greatly in value according to their condition, but not many particularly good Holmesian toys have been produced, and any older toys thus have a good rarity value.

MORIARTY, WATSON & HOLMES *(from left to right). Popular wall sculptures made by Bossons of Congleton.*

Ceramics and Models

Numerous mugs and plates have been issued to commemorate various anniversaries connected with Holmes and Doyle, and most of these have increased their value very rapidly. This is especially true of the limited editions, with some of the 1987 Centenary mugs, originally priced at around £10 ($20), selling in 1990 for more than double that price. Models of Holmes, Watson and Moriarty have always been popular, but the quality of production has varied a great deal. Production numbers have tended to be low, and so current prices are correspondingly high.

THE SCOTTISH HOLMES *(far left).*

THE JAPANESE HOLMES *(left). The inspiration for this red-headed statuette of Holmes, made in Japan, is unknown.*

PORTRAYALS OF HOLMES *The limited edition plate (far left) features some of the actors who have played the master sleuth. Key: 1. Basil Rathbone; 2. John Barrymore; 3. Arthur Wontner; 4. Eille Norwood; 5. Kenneth MacMillan; 6. John Wood; 7. John Neville; 8. Alan Wheatley; 9. Robert Stephens; 10. Clive Brook; 11. H. Hamilton Stewart; 12. Geoffrey Edwards; 13. H.A. Saintsbury; 14. William Gillette; 15. Carleton Hobbs; 16. Peter Cushing; 17. Christopher Plummer; 18. Douglas Wilmer; 19. Jeremy Brett; 20. Nigel Bruce (Dr Watson).*

HOLMES IN BRONZE *from the Sherlock Holmes Museum in London. The bust was made by the British sculptor Martin Lorenz.*

HOLMESIAN TEAPOT (*near right*). *A fine example of Sherlockian kitsch from the Far East.*

HOLMES DUTCH DOLL (*right*). *Early twentieth-century hand-made Dutch doll loosely based on the Paget illustrations.*

SHERLOCK HOLMES PUZZLE, (*far right*), *Early cigarette card from Gallaher's.*

WALL RELIEF (*near right*). *The sculpture is made entirely of different metals.*

BLUE MUG (*right*) *was from the former Moriarty's Baker Street Tube Station Pub in London.*

VARSITY POSTER (*right*). *Holmes quickly became a vehicle for advertising as this 1907 cigarette poster illustrates.*

JOHN PLAYER & SONS CIGARETTE CARD (*far right*). *No.21 of a series of 25 cards entitled "Characters from Fiction", this illustration is based on an original one by H.M. Brock.*

Advertisements

Holmes has always been a popular figure in advertisements, and some of these can be obtained literally for nothing, although dealers do charge considerable sums for some of them. Again, it is worthwhile keeping the whole magazine if it contains a Holmesian advertisement. A specialist form of advertising was the cigarette card, and

Holmes appears in some of these. The Alexander Boguslavsky set of 25 Doylean characters will cost at least £50 ($100) for the green-backed set, and £70 ($140) for the scarcer black-backed version, and dealers in such cards are all well aware of the values. Holmes has also appeared on beer mats, and there are specialist dealers for these, with prices being around £1 ($2) for each mat (preferably without any alcoholic content!).

GOVERNMENT WEALTH WARNING
Collecting Holmesiana
Can Severely Damage
Your Bank Balance

CHESTERFIELD HOLMES *(left)*. *Basil Rathbone advertising the cigarettes.*

"THE ORIGINAL SHERLOCK HOLMES" PIPE *(below)*. *An elementary advertisement for Peterson of Dublin.*

Collier's

Household Number for November

Sherlock Holmes

In this Number Solves
The Mystery of

The
Norwood Builder

THE CANON

Summaries of The Stories

AN INTRODUCTION TO THE CASE SUMMARIES

These summaries are in no way intended to provide alternatives to reading the cases themselves, for nothing could compete with the pleasures given by the original cases. It is also most strongly recommended that none of these summaries should be read before the original case, for that could easily spoil much of the enjoyment.

The main purpose of the summaries is to provide a version of how each case might be seen, in order to have something with which to compare and contrast one's own interpretation. Part of the greatness of the cases is that they seem to be capable of supplying something to many different types of readers, and it is hoped that these summaries will help each reader to identify something of that for themselves.

Included with each summary are some narrative points of particular interest in each case, as well as an indication of the publishing history of the story. There is also a listing of the major characters in each case, as it can often be difficult to recall some of these. All of the character names are not given, as there are over 400 of them

in the Canon! Holmes and Watson are not mentioned in the lists of characters, and very often Watson's name is omitted from parts of the summary, where it is obvious or unimportant to the facts of the case that he was present.

The cases are listed here in the chronological order in which they were first published.

HOLMES AS ILLUSTRATED BY FRANK WILES *(opposite). The frontispiece to the first instalment of* The Valley of Fear. *It was the only illustration in colour to accompany a Sherlock Holmes story in* The Strand Magazine.

A REVERIE *(left). Illustrating some of the earlier cases that appeared in* The Strand Magazine.

CIGARETTE CARDS *(far left): Man with the Twisted Lip, King of Bohemia, and Mary Morstan.*

THE STRAND MAGAZINE *(below), September 1914, cover containing the first instalment of* The Valley of Fear.

A STUDY IN SCARLET

First published: *Beeton's Christmas Annual* in November 1887
Main Characters: Stamford, Inspectors Gregson and Lestrade, Enoch Drebber,
Joseph Stangerson, Lieutenant Charpentier, John Ferrier, Lucy Ferrier, Jefferson Hope

Watson informs us of something of his own background, and then recalls the occasion when he was first introduced to Sherlock Holmes at Bart's Hospital by his old medical colleague Stamford. He moved into 221B Baker Street with Holmes and discovered a little of Holmes's interests and abilities before Holmes informed him that he was the world's first private consulting detective. Watson is invited to accompany Holmes in the investigation of the death of Enoch Drebber at an empty house in Lauriston Gardens, where Inspectors Gregson and Lestrade are officiating. Holmes minutely examines the approaches and interior of the house, then quite unexpectedly declares that Drebber has been poisoned and gives a detailed description of the probable assailant. He then publicly advertises the finding in the street of a woman's wedding ring, although this ring was actually found under Drebber's body. The "lady" who collects the ring evades Holmes's pursuit, and Holmes realizes that it was actually a young man.

Drebber, an American, had apparently been travelling with a private secretary,

THE 1987 DUNHILL PIPE. *The limited edition pipe and case were made to commemorate the centenary of* A Study in Scarlet.

Joseph Stangerson, during their visit to England. Gregson informs Holmes that he has arrested a Lieutenant Charpentier, who had quarrelled violently with Drebber over the latter's insulting behaviour to Charpentier's sister, but Lestrade then arrives to say that Stangerson had been stabbed to death in a hotel at a time when Charpentier was already under arrest. Lestrade had found two pills in Stangerson's room, and Holmes feeds half of one of these to an ailing dog, but with no result. He then feeds half the other pill to the dog and it perishes immediately. The leader of Holmes's band of street urchins, the "Baker Street Irregulars, arrives with a cab, and when the driver attempts to help with Holmes's box Holmes handcuffs him and announces that the driver is Jefferson Hope, the murderer of Drebber and Stangerson.

It is then revealed that John Ferrier and his adopted daughter, Lucy, had, many years previously, been rescued by the Mormons whilst they were travelling across America. Ferrier had settled with the Mormons in Salt Lake City, but he had not accepted all their ways. Lucy had later met Jefferson Hope, a cattleman and hunter, when he passed through Salt Lake City, and she fell in love with him. Her father had been warned that Lucy must marry either Drebber or Stangerson, and had been given one month in which to decide. He and Lucy escaped with Hope when the latter returned just before the marriage date. In flight, Hope returned from a short hunting trip to find Ferrier dead and Lucy captured by the Mormons. On returning to Salt Lake City he found that Lucy had been forced to marry Drebber, but she then pined away and died within a month. Hope had taken the wedding ring from Lucy's finger before her funeral and vowed vengeance on Drebber and Stangerson. He had gone to the mines to recover his health and wealth before tackling Drebber and Stangerson, but had later found that they had left Utah. Hope had eventually tracked them to London, where he began work as a cab driver.

Hope had found Drebber in a drunken state and taken him to Lauriston Gardens where he had confronted him. To test the providence of his actions, Hope had offered Drebber a choice between two pills, one of which was poisoned. Drebber had taken the poisoned one and Hope the other. When Hope had later attempted to do the same with Stangerson, there had been a fight and Stangerson had been stabbed. Hope reveals that he has a faulty artery, from which he is expected to die within days, and although he is taken to prison he does die before the trial.

Holmes explains that he had solved the case by identifying and concentrating on the most important points. The wedding ring found under the body had suggested that a woman was involved, and Holmes had enquired of the American police as to whether there was anything unusual about Drebber's marriage. He had been informed that Drebber had sought protection against a Jefferson Hope. The footprints at Lauriston Gardens had indicated that Drebber's assailant had probably been a cab driver, and Holmes had then set the Irregulars to find a cab driver named Hope. As was so

A STUDY IN SCARLET CENTENARY POSTCARD (*above*). *On the left is the first illustration of Sherlock Holmes, by D.H. Friston.*

often to happen, the case concludes with the official police receiving the credit for solving the crime.

This case is, of course, of prime importance for introducing Watson, Holmes and the methods by which Holmes works. Perhaps the main reason why it was difficult to sell the narrative originally was that it is too long, consisting essentially of a good short story which is made overlong by the excessively and unnecessarily detailed description of the American interlude. Watson was to reduce this problem, but not get rid of it entirely, when he related the Indian details in his next recorded case, *The Sign of Four*. In spite of this problem, this first case provides a magnificent introduction to all that is to follow, and we constantly find that we refer back to the information contained in this case when we consider the later ones. Watson's listing of Holmes's talents, or lack of them, inevitably makes us consider Holmes's development as his career progresses. It is with this case that we begin to attempt to cope with such diverse questions as the location of Watson's wound. It is also here that we meet that epitome of the official force, Inspector Lestrade, who even manages to cause us difficulties over whether his name is pronounced "Lestrayed" or "Lestraad", and whether the accent is on the first or second syllable of this name. With such an introduction, the game is certainly afoot!

1953 COLOUR VERSION OF *A STUDY IN SCARLET* (*left*).

THE SIGN OF FOUR

First published: *Lippincott's Monthly Magazine* in February 1890
under the title *The Sign of the Four*
Main Characters: Mary Morstan, Captain Morstan, Major Sholto, Thaddeus Sholto,
Bartholomew Sholto, Jonathan Small, Inspector Athelney Jones, Tonga

The narrative begins with Holmes taking cocaine to relieve the boredom of inactivity, but he soon becomes totally engrossed when Miss Mary Morstan arrives at 221B to inform him about her situation. Her father, Captain Morstan, had disappeared ten years previously on returning to London from duty in India. For each of the last six years she had received a large pearl by post, and she had now been asked to meet her benefactor. Holmes discovers that Captain Morstan's only friend in London, Major Sholto, had mysteriously died a few days before the first pearl had been sent and that Morstan had had some connection with a group of men known as "The Four".

Holmes and Watson accompany Mary to her rendezvous, where one of the twin sons of Major Sholto, Thaddeus, explains that his father had illegally obtained possession of the Agra treasure, with Morstan's assistance, whilst they were commanding a penal colony in the Andaman Islands. When Morstan returned to England he had died from a weak heart whilst arguing over his share of the treasure, and Sholto had secretly disposed of the body. On his deathbed, Sholto had asked his sons to ensure that Mary got her share of the treasure, but then died of shock on seeing a wooden-legged man at his window, before he could reveal the treasure's hiding place. A note reading "The sign of the four" was later found on his body. Thaddeus had been sending Mary the pearls from the only piece of the treasure that was not hidden, but his brother, Bartholomew, had apparently just discovered the rest of the treasure.

THE SLEUTH (*above*). *One of Royal Doulton's best selling toby jugs.*

SOMETHING'S AMISS. *Eille Norwood in* The Sign of Four, *1923. Humberston Wright plays the corpse.*

Holmes, Watson, Mary and Thaddeus travel to Bartholomew's house, where they find him dead, with a poisoned thorn in his neck and a note reading "The sign of the four". The treasure is also gone. Holmes finds the marks of a one-legged man and what appears to be a bare-footed child. He deduces that the man is Jonathan Small, since that was the name of the only Englishman included in a listing of "The Four" found in Morstan's papers. Holmes follows their trail and finds that they have boarded a launch called the *Aurora*.

In the meantime, Inspector Athelney Jones arrests Thaddeus and detains most of Bartholomew's household in connection with the murder. Holmes sends out his band of street urchins, the Baker Street Irregulars, to search for the *Aurora*. He discovers that amongst the Andaman Islanders there are some very short savages who use poisoned darts to kill their victims, and concludes that the footprints of the "child" must have been those of such an Andaman savage. Watson keeps Mary informed of proceedings and records an increasing affection for her, but remains constrained by the thought of her potential inheritance.

Holmes eventually locates the *Aurora*, and when Small sails he is chased by Holmes, Watson and Jones in a police launch. When the savage attempts to use his blow-pipe, he

THE INTENSITY OF HOLMES. *Arthur Wontner in the 1932 film* The Sign of Four. *Wonter was one of the more successful actors to portray Holmes, closely resembling a Paget illustration despite the ill-fitting toupee.*

is shot, and Small is then caught. Watson takes the treasure box to Mary, but they discover that Small has emptied the contents into the Thames. As Mary is no longer to be rich, Watson admits that he loves her, and she reciprocates. The case ends with Watson announcing that he is about to be married, Jones getting the credit for arresting Small, and Holmes returning to his cocaine-bottle.

This case has the most notorious example of Holmes's drug abuse, but, as has been explained elsewhere, this habit declined when he became more famous and had better things to occupy him. It provides some excellent examples of his deductive abilities, including the incident where we find that Watson once had an older brother. There are also many indications of Holmes's sense of humour, and of his delight in being involved with something challenging. There is a great deal of information provided about Watson, and especially about his romantic inclinations. Watson's feelings for Mary are extremely well recorded, as are Holmes's lack of enthusiasm for the loss of a colleague in this manner. There are numerous problems in the case, such as the nature of the savage Tonga's poison, which seems to have almost magical powers, but which does not appear to exist in any recorded poison.

THE SIGN OF FOUR

A. CONAN DOYLE

Who murdered Sholto? The last and highest court of appeal in detection – Sherlock Holmes – was roused to solve that problem – and solved it.

2/- NET

JOHN MURRAY **Arthur Conan Doyle**

DUST COVER *for the John Murray "two-shilling novels" edition of 1924.*

A SCANDAL IN BOHEMIA

First published: *The Strand Magazine* in July 1891
Main Characters: Irene Adler, the King of Bohemia

The King of Bohemia engages Holmes to retrieve a mildly compromising photograph from the King's former mistress, Irene Adler, since any scandal might jeopardize the King's forthcoming marriage. Holmes follows Irene and becomes involved as a witness at her marriage to Godfrey Norton. He later gains entry to her house, disguised as an elderly clergyman who is injured whilst attempting to rescue Irene from ruffians hired by himself. He tricks Irene into revealing the location of the photograph when Watson starts a fire scare from outside the house. When Holmes returns to Irene's house with the King the next day, however, he finds that she has discovered his ruse and already left for the Continent with her husband. She has left a note for Holmes, explaining that she would never use the photograph, unless threatened by the King, and she has also left another photograph of herself in the hiding place. Holmes claimed this photograph as part of his reward from the King, and thereafter always referred to Irene as "The Woman".

This case has generated numerous theories about Holmes's attitude towards women. The respect which he demonstrates for Irene who, to some extent, bettered him, contrasts markedly with his more often expressed suspicion and dislike for women in general. Watson records that this was just an intellectual admiration, but the keeping of the photograph implies more, although any emotions were certainly kept well suppressed. Holmes also shows that he was no respecter of mere rank, since he is quite openly rude to the King at times. The case shows something of Holmes's sense of humour, including an outburst of laughter which contrasts with the saturnine appearance more often described by Watson.

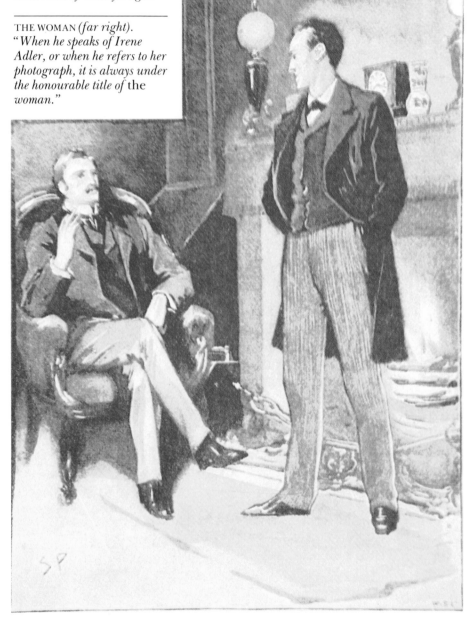

"THEN HE STOOD BEFORE THE FIRE." *Holmes assessing a heavier and married Watson. Illustrated by Sidney Paget.*

THE WOMAN *(far right).* "*When he speaks of Irene Adler, or when he refers to her photograph, it is always under the honourable title of* the woman."

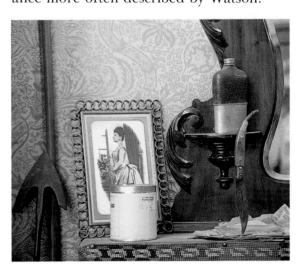

THE RED-HEADED LEAGUE

First published: *The Strand Magazine* in August 1891
Main Characters: Jabez Wilson, Vincent Spaulding, John Clay, Peter Jones

The red-headed Jabez Wilson informs Holmes that he has been employed for some eight weeks, part-time, in copying out the *Encyclopaedia Britannica*. His employer has been The Red-Headed League, a philanthropic organization for men with red hair, which paid him well but insisted upon him working alone in an office from 10AM until 2PM each day. He had been informed about this job by his assistant, Vincent Spaulding, who ran Wilson's pawnbroking business whilst the latter was working at the League's office. Wilson had arrived at the office that morning to find a notice declaring the League dissolved.

Holmes asks for further details about Spaulding, then visits the area of Wilson's shop and confirms Spaulding's true identity as that of a notorious criminal called John Clay. Holmes persuades Peter Jones, a police agent, and the local bank manager to hide themselves with Holmes and Watson in the vaults of the bank behind Wilson's shop, where there are large, temporary deposits of gold coins. Clay and his accomplice complete a tunnel into the vault and are arrested. Holmes had deduced that Clay was decoying Wilson away from the shop, and confirmed that he was tunnelling by the marks on the knees of Clay's trousers. He found that the direction of the tunnel was to the rear of the shop by the absence of any hollow sound when he tapped the pavement in front of the shop with his stick.

This case provides some excellent examples of Holmes's deductive abilities, especially with the classical introductory analysis of Wilson's background, very much in the style of Dr Bell, the tutor of Watson's Literary Agent, Dr Doyle. The suggestion can be made that Peter Jones is a Watsonian mistake for Athelney Jones, especially as the Sholto case is specifically mentioned. There is also a question of the meaning of Clay shouting to his accomplice that he will "swing for it", as the crime they are committing is certainly not a capital one. He may

have been acknowledging the fact that one of his earlier crimes was punishable by hanging, or, possibly, that he may have already murdered Wilson to facilitate the final phase of the robbery.

"MR. MERRYWEATHER STOPPED TO LIGHT A LANTERN." *The bank director accompanies Holmes, Watson and Jones as they wait for the robbers.*

"HE CURLED HIMSELF UP IN HIS CHAIR." *To contemplate the case (below) as does Jeremy Brett for the Granada Television series (below left).*

A CASE OF IDENTITY

First published: *The Strand Magazine* in September 1891
Main Characters: Mary Sutherland, Mr Windibank, Hosmer Angel

Miss Mary Sutherland reports that she lives at home with her mother and her step-father, Mr Windibank, the latter being only slightly older than herself. She gives her small but comfortable inheritance to her step-father. Whilst Mr Windibank was away on business she had met Mr Hosmer Angel at the annual Gasfitters' Ball, and he had courted her. When her step-father returned he banned Angel from the house without ever meeting him. She continued to see Angel whenever Windibank was away, but his visits were usually at night, because he was shy. He also had weak eyes, which

necessitated wearing dark glasses, and a throat condition which resulted in very soft speech. He insisted on being written to only through a post office address. Mary had promised to stay faithful to him, whatever happened, then on the way to their wedding, Angel had disappeared.

Holmes warns Mary that she should forget Angel, but she insist that he should investigate. Holmes is later visited by Windibank and accuses him of being Angel, a deception designed to maintain control of Mary's income. Holmes had deduced this largely from Angel's letters being typed on Windibank's typewriter, from the disguising techniques of the dark glasses and soft voice, and the fact that the two men never appeared together. Holmes accepts that Windibank's activities are not actionable, but threatens him with a horse-whipping if they continue. He also confides to Watson that Mary Sutherland would probably never accept the true explanation.

There is no really satisfactory conclusion to this case, mainly because it is one of several cases in the Canon where it is claimed that no actual crime takes place. Although Holmes may have been wrong about the legality of Windibank's activities, his conclusion about Mary was probably correct, which in turn would mean that Windibank would achieve his intentions if no legal action was used to cause a breaking up of the home. The case includes a reference to a vice which Holmes may have shared with his brother Mycroft, with Holmes offering a snuff-box to Watson. As it was a recent present from the King of Bohemia, however, Holmes may merely have been showing it off to Watson, as it is never mentioned again.

"I FOUND SHERLOCK HOLMES HALF ASLEEP." *But don't be fooled. This Paget illustration is not of a lazy Holmes but one who has just solved the case and is awaiting the culprit.*

THE BOSCOMBE VALLEY MYSTERY

First published: *The Strand Magazine* in October 1891
Main Characters: John Turner, Alice Turner, Charles McCarthy, James McCarthy,
Inspector Lestrade

John Turner had purchased a large estate in Herefordshire after making money in Australia, and he later let one of his farms to Charles McCarthy, whom he had met in Australia. McCarthy's son, James, had been seen arguing fiercely with his father near Boscombe Pool. After the quarrel, hearing some cries, James had returned to the pool to find his father dying from a head wound. The father's last words appeared to be something about a rat. The son was arrested and Holmes was called in by Lestrade to assist.

John Turner's daughter, Alice, attempts to persuade Holmes of James's innocence, and informs him that her own father is very ill. Holmes visits James in gaol and discovers that James is in love with Alice but secretly married to a barmaid in Bristol, although that lady has revealed that James is not in fact her only husband. The next day Holmes examines the scene of the crime. From the clues there he describes the killer, and suggests that the dying reference was not to a rat but to Ballarat in Australia. Holmes is visited by John Turner, who admits killing McCarthy because he had been blackmailing him over the fact that Turner had been a member of the Ballarat Gang of robbers. As Turner is dying from a disease, Holmes does not have him arrested but arranges for the release of James.

In this case, Holmes is described as wearing "a long gray travelling cloak and close-fitting cloth cap", and it was from this that Sidney Paget produced the hooded coat and deerstalker which became so much a part of the Holmes image. Holmes demonstrates a fallibility which makes him rather more human, when he misattributes the quotation of "There, but for the grace of God, goes . . ." to the seventeenth century's Richard Baxter, when it is a paraphrase of the words of the sixteenth century's John Bradford. Holmes's decision not to have Turner arrested is one of many examples of him interpreting the law selectively.

"WE HAD THE CARRIAGE TO OURSELVES." *After disrupting Watson's breakfast, Holmes takes the doctor on a journey west to Herefordshire to unravel the mystery of the Boscombe Valley.*

THE FIVE ORANGE PIPS

First published: *The Strand Magazine* in November 1891
Main Characters: John Openshaw, Joseph Openshaw, Elias Openshaw,
Captain James Calhoun

John Openshaw arrives at 221B late on a stormy night. He relates that his father, Joseph, has retired comfortably, and that his uncle, Elias, had made a considerable fortune in America before returning to live in Sussex because of his objections to negro emancipation in America. Some four years previously, Elias had received an envelope from India, marked with "KKK" and containing five orange pips. He had imme-

"HIS EYES BENT UPON THE GLOW OF THE FIRE." Holmes contemplates the mystery of the ominous fruit seeds.

diately burned some papers from a locked box, then made out a will leaving everything to Joseph. Shortly afterwards he was found dead in a shallow pond. Some years after this, John's father had received a similar envelope from Dublin with an additional note saying "Put the papers on the sun dial". Subsequently, he had been found dying of a shattered skull after a fall into a chalk-pit. John had now received a similar demand from London.

Holmes discovers that "KKK" stands for the Ku Klux Klan, an American racist organization which warns men that it has condemned with orange pips. He also notes that all the demands came from seaports, and that a major disruption of the KKK in America had coincided with Elias's return to England. That night, John's body is recovered from the Thames. Holmes ascertains that the murderer was Captain James Calhoun of the *Lone Star*, because the posting dates of the letters coincided with visits of his ship to the particular ports. Holmes sends five orange pips to Calhoun, but the *Lone Star* is lost at sea on its next voyage.

This case is one of Holmes's failures, in that he loses his client before he concludes the case, but this also makes the Canon more realistic, in that no-one could meet with success in all of the numerous cases which Holmes investigates. Watson's own susceptibility to human weakness is also indicated here, with his condemnation of Holmes as a "self-poisoner" by tobacco, even though he himself admits to smoking strong tobacco before joining Holmes at 221B.

THE MAN WITH THE TWISTED LIP

First published: *The Strand Magazine* in December 1891
Main Characters: Neville St Clair, Mrs St Clair, Hugh Boone, Inspector Bradstreet

At the request of his wife's friend, Mrs Whitney, Watson recovers her husband from an opium den, and there finds Holmes, in disguise, searching for a missing Neville St Clair. After despatching Whitney home, Holmes and Watson travel to St Clair's house to question his wife. St Clair journeyed to London supposedly on business each day, but whilst visiting a riverside London location Mrs St Clair was surprised to see her husband at a window above the opium den. After the police had been called, the room was searched. The only man in the room was a beggar called Hugh Boone, who had a badly disfigured face. Blood stains were found, and St Clair's jacket which had been recovered from the river weighed down with numerous coins.

Holmes informs Mrs St Clair that he believes her husband to be dead, but finds that she has just received a reassuring note and his signet ring. The next morning Holmes drives to Bow Street police station where Boone is being kept, and, accompanied by Inspector Bradstreet, he scrubs Boone's face to reveal that he is actually St Clair, who had been earning a comfortable living through begging. St Clair promises never to use the disguise again.

"THE PIPE WAS STILL BETWEEN HIS LIPS." *Watson awakes to find that Holmes has been up all night smoking shag and analyzing the clues.*

This is another of the cases in which there is no real crime committed. It is also the case in which Mrs Watson calls her husband James, to the lasting delight of Watsonian theorists everywhere. Grave doubts have been caused over Watson's suggestion that Boone's make-up be removed with a sponge and cold water; since Holmes was such an expert with make-up he would surely have gone to the police station with an appropriate removal cream.

THE ADVENTURE OF THE BLUE CARBUNCLE

First published: *The Strand Magazine* in January 1892
Main Characters: Peterson, Henry Baker, John Horner, James Ryder

Whilst returning home from a Christmas celebration, Peterson, the commissionaire, witnesses a man attacked by roughs. The man drops his hat and the goose he is carrying whilst trying to defend himself, and then accidentally breaks a window with his stick at which point Peterson intervenes – causing the roughs as well as the startled man to flee. Holmes advises Peterson to eat the goose, then he analyses the hat, which he discovers belongs to Henry Baker.

Peterson later discovers the Blue Carbuncle, a huge gem stolen from the Duchess of Morcar, in the goose and brings it to Holmes, who recognizes it. John Horner, a plumber who was working in the hotel room from which the stone was stolen, has been arrested on the evidence of James

"SEE WHAT MY WIFE FOUND IN ITS CROP!" *The commissionaire hands over the precious stone after his wife found something hard in the bird's gullet (above).*

" 'HAVE MERCY!' HE SHRIEKED." *Ryder importunes Holmes for leniency (above right).*

"HE BURST INTO CONVULSIVE SOBBING." *And Holmes lets him leave (right). A moment of sympathy from the consulting detective?*

Ryder, the hotel attendant. Holmes advertises for the owner of the hat and, when finding him innocent, replaces his lost bird with another. Holmes then traces the supplier of the original bird, where he finds James Ryder also looking for the supplier. On being confronted, Ryder admits to stealing the stone and stuffing it into a goose as a hiding place, after which he had taken the wrong goose. Holmes lets Ryder off with a severe cautioning and the stone is returned to its owner, with Peterson getting the offered reward and Horner being released.

This case involves an extended and brilliant example of Holmes's deductive powers in his analysis of Baker's hat. This story is also another example of Holmes acting as his own court of law, in deciding Ryder's fate.

It can be suggested that here Holmes readily accepts a form of redistributing wealth, in that he states that the Duchess can easily afford the large reward given to Peterson.

THE ADVENTURE OF THE SPECKLED BAND

First published: *The Strand Magazine* in February 1892
Main Characters: Helen Stoner, Julia Stoner, Grimesby Roylott

Miss Helen Stoner informs Holmes that her late mother had bequeathed a large income to herself, her twin sister, and her step-father, Dr Grimesby Roylott, with whom Helen and her sister had continued to live after their mother's death. Julia had become engaged two years previously, and had informed Helen that she had heard a mysterious whistling sound at night. Shortly afterwards Julia died, muttering "the speckled band". Helen had recently become betrothed, and had been moved by her stepfather into Julia's old room, where she too had heard a whistling sound.

After Helen's departure from 221B, Roylott arrives to warn Holmes to stay out of his affairs, but Holmes and Watson later travel to Roylott's house to examine the fatal bedroom. That night they secretly occupy the room and find a snake crawling down a false bell-rope towards the bed. Holmes drives the snake back into the adjoining room, where it kills Roylott, who had trained it to seek out victims and then be recalled by a whistle. He had tried to kill the sisters to prevent them marrying and taking away their inheritance.

This case is the one which has most frequently been voted the best of the short Holmesian stories. It certainly has every element of drama and suspense, but it also has one of the most contorted methods of murdering someone ever invented. It shows Holmes's disregard for the opinions of others: when Roylott bends a poker to show his strength, Holmes does not bend it straight in front of Roylott, but waits until he has gone. His verbal responses to Roylott's threatening bluster certainly demonstrate a superb coolness. There are some difficulties however with the creatures in this case since there is no such snake as a swamp adder.

THE ADVENTURE OF THE ENGINEER'S THUMB

First published: *The Strand Magazine* in March 1892
Main Characters: Victor Hatherley, Colonel Lysander Stark, Mr Ferguson/
Dr Becher, Elise, Inspector Bradstreet

Victor Hatherley, a hydraulic engineer, is brought to Watson's surgery having lost a thumb in a murderous attack. Watson takes Hatherley to Holmes, where the engineer states that he had been asked by Colonel Stark to investigate a faulty hydraulic press at his house. Hatherley was taken to the house by a long route from Reading railway station, in the dark, and was introduced to Stark's manager, Mr Ferguson. He was secretly warned to leave the house by a lady called Elise. Hatherley soon discovered the fault, but also found that the machine was being used to press counterfeit coins, and was thereupon locked inside the press with the ram ready to crush him. The lady freed him, but while hanging from a window ledge he was attacked by Stark who severed Hatherley's thumb with a cleaver.

Holmes recalls that another hydraulic engineer had disappeared mysteriously a year ago. On reaching Reading with Hatherley and Inspector Bradstreet, Holmes deduces that the house is close to the station, and that Hatherley had been driven in circles on his previous visit. There they discover the charred remains of the house. They also find that the householder, Mr Ferguson, who is known locally as Dr Becher, has fled with the rest of the gang, and they are never heard of again.

This is an extremely unsatisfactory case, in that the criminals appear to suffer only the inconvenience of having to move their location. There is the common problem in this case of a police officer apparently accompanying Holmes outside of the officer's district, but this time it could be suggested that the plain clothes officer who accompanies them might have been previously called to London from the Reading area. There are differences in the text between *The Strand Magazine* and the book version, in connection with the position of Hatherley's hands on the windowsill, which can be used to explain how Stark actually managed to reach Hatherley's thumb whilst he was hanging there. The Paget drawing, however, also shows how it could have been done.

THE ADVENTURE OF THE NOBLE BACHELOR

First published: *The Strand Magazine* in April 1892
Main Characters: Lord Robert St Simon, Hatty Doran, Flora Miller, Frank Moulton, Inspector Lestrade

CONAN DOYLE CHARACTERS

LESTRADE

After the wedding of Lord Robert St Simon and Hatty Doran, the daughter of an American millionaire, the bride had disappeared. Flora Miller, who had tried earlier to force her way into the reception, had been arrested by Lestrade. St Simon calls on Holmes and admits that he had been very friendly with Flora, and recalls that at the wedding Hatty had been handed flowers by an unknown man, but had dropped them. Holmes states that he has solved the case but does not yet know the location of the missing bride.

Hatty's dress is then found in the Serpentine, with a note written on the back of a hotel bill arranging a rendezvous. Holmes invites St Simon to supper, where they are joined by Hatty and Frank Moulton, her husband by an earlier marriage who had been thought dead. Holmes had traced him by checking the hotels which charged the high prices shown on the bill. St Simon departs, feeling insulted.

This is yet another case in which no intentional crime is committed, and we have another example of Holmes's dislike for snobbery. Here, as in other cases, there are also, quite correctly, objections to the way in which Holmes addresses nobility. St Simon is referred to as "Lord St Simon", whereas, as the second son of a duke (the Duke of Balmoral), he should actually be referred to as Lord Robert St Simon or simply as Lord Robert. Similarly, it should be Lady Robert, not Lady St Simon.

THE ADVENTURE OF THE BERYL CORONET

First published: *The Strand Magazine* in May 1892
Main Characters: Alexander Holder, Arthur Holder, Sir George Burnwell, Mary

Alexander Holder, a banker, arrives at 221B to inform Holmes that he has loaned £50,000 to a client against the security of the famous Beryl Coronet. He had taken it home, where he lived with his son, Arthur, and his niece, Mary. Arthur, under the bad influence of a Sir George Burnwell, had previously asked for money to pay off gambling debts, and had been refused. Awakened in the early hours, Holder had found Arthur holding the coronet, from which three stones were missing, and so Arthur had been arrested.

Holmes examines the house and deduces that the coronet must have been broken outside the house. The next day, Mary disappears. Holmes asks for £4,000 and produces the missing gems. From footprints in the garden, Holmes deduced that Mary had met Sir George and given him the coronet, but Arthur had retrieved it, unknowingly having snapped off the three stones in the struggle. Arthur had refused to inform on Mary and had gone to prison for her. Holmes retrieved the stones from a dealer at £1,000 each, and charged another £1,000 for his services.

With his often repeated claim that he does his job for its own sake, one must assume that Holmes's large fee in this case was a reasonable charge against a man who was foolish enough to place something so valuable in a weak bureau at home, rather than in the safe at the bank. Much consternation has been caused by the reference at the start of this case to a bow window at 221B, since there were no houses with bow windows in Baker Street. Bow-topped windows, however, were very popular at that time.

THE ADVENTURE OF THE COPPER BEECHES

First published: *The Strand Magazine* in June 1892
Main Characters: Violet Hunter, Jephro Rucastle, Mrs Rucastle, Alice Rucastle, Mr Fowler, Carlo the mastiff

Miss Violet Hunter asks for Holmes's advice over accepting an appointment as a governess at the Copper Beeches near Winchester. Her potential employer, Jephro Rucastle, was offering high wages but required her to cut off her long hair and to wear such dresses as he and his wife might decide. After initially refusing she had been offered an even higher wage by Rucastle. Holmes promises help if needed, and is later called to Winchester. Violet explains that the adult daughter of the house had apparently gone to America because of an aversion to Rucastle, her step-father. Violet had cut her hair and been made to sit in a window wearing a particular blue dress. When she found that a young man was observing her, she was told to signal him to go away. Later she discovered that someone was locked in hidden rooms.

Holmes concludes that Violet has been tricked into impersonating Rucastle's

"RUNNING UP, I BLEW ITS BRAINS OUT." *Watson disposing of a vengeful pet.*

gives chase, but is savaged by his own half-starved mastiff. The daughter, Alice, had been held to control her rights to the estate, but she had been rescued by the mysterious man, Mr Fowler, who then marries her. Miss Hunter moves to a school in Walsall.

Some of the marks of admiration which Holmes expresses for Violet suggest to Watson that Holmes has deeper interests in the lady, but he is eventually disappointed. Once again, the interest appears to be an intellectual appreciation rather than a romantic one. Some have taken Holmes's casual reference to the advice which "he might have given to his own sister" to indicate that he had such a sister, but one might expect Watson to have questioned this, if not on this occasion then when he discovered that Holmes had a brother.

step-daughter, and that the young man is the daughter's friend. Holmes enters the house when Rucastle is away, and finds the hidden rooms empty. Rucastle returns and

THE ADVENTURE OF SILVER BLAZE

First published: *The Strand Magazine* in December 1892
Main Characters: Colonel Ross, John Straker, Fitzroy Simpson, Inspector Gregory, Silver Blaze

Holmes is invited by Inspector Gregory to visit Colonel Ross's King's Pyland stables on Dartmoor. A stable boy, Ned Hunter, had been drugged after chasing off a gentleman tout, Fitzroy Simpson, and Silver Blaze, the favourite for the Wessex Cup, was missing. The horse's trainer, John Straker, had been found dead with a crushed skull on the nearby moor. After examining the death scene, Holmes follows horse-prints to a rival stable, where he talks confidentially with the manager, Silas Brown. Holmes then assures Colonel Ross that his missing horse will run.

At the race, near Winchester, an apparently different horse runs, but it is revealed to be the disguised Silver Blaze, which Brown had concealed after finding it loose on the moor. Straker had drugged the stable lad, then taken the horse onto the moor to make it lame, but the horse became frightened and kicked Straker fatally in the head. Holmes had discovered that Straker

"BE OFF!" *Meeting with some uncooperative horse lovers.*

had needed money to support his mistress, and had deduced Straker's consequent actions from the clues on Dartmoor.

The levels of deduction exhibited by Holmes in this case are very high. He amuses himself by not revealing the facts that he has discovered particularly at the expense of Colonel Ross, largely because the latter was rude to him. It is in this case that Holmes is described as wearing "an ear-flapped travelling cap", and it would be difficult to disagree with Paget illustrating this as the now-famous deerstalker.

"HOLMES WAS EXTREMELY PLEASED." *The sleuth finds interesting clues in the ailments of sheep (above).*

"HE LAID HIS HAND UPON THE GLOSSY NECK." *Once again Holmes identifies the killer only this time it is a horse acting in self-defence. No charges were filed (left).*

THE ADVENTURE OF THE CARDBOARD BOX

First published: *The Strand Magazine* in January 1893
Main Characters: Susan Cushing, Mary Cushing, Sarah Cushing, James Browner, Alec Fairbairn, Inspector Lestrade

Holmes, Watson and Lestrade visit Susan Cushing, who has been sent two human ears in a cardboard box. Susan relates that a ship's steward, James Browner, had married her youngest sister, Mary, but later took to drink and quarrelled with Mary and her other sister, Sarah, who was then living with the married couple. On attempting to visit Sarah they find that she is ill, and Holmes arranges for Lestrade to arrest Browner when he arrives in London. Browner confesses that Sarah had made advances to him, but was spurned and then encouraged Mary to suspect him. Mary later became involved with another sailor, Alec Fairbairn. Browner followed his wife and Fairbairn to New Brighton and murdered them. He cut an ear from each body and sent them to where he thought that Sarah Cushing was living, but only Susan lived there by then.

Perhaps the most remarkable point about this case, apart from its gruesomeness, is its publishing history. The case was not included in the collected edition of the second set of cases from *The Strand Magazine*, *The Memoirs of Sherlock Holmes*, possibly because Watson's Literary Agent regretted the initial publication of a story involving a married woman's indiscretion. Perhaps the social climate was considered to have changed by 1917, for the case was included then in the collection, *His Last Bow*. However, the mind-reading episode which introduces the case was transferred completely to the earlier *The Resident Patient*, although the seasons referred to in that case do not coincide with the ones mentioned in this episode. When *The Complete Sherlock Holmes Short Stories* was published in 1928, the mind-reading episode was returned to *The Cardboard Box*, although the American *Complete Sherlock Holmes* edition now has this episode in both *The Cardboard Box* and *The Resident Patient*.

THE ADVENTURE OF THE YELLOW FACE

First published: *The Strand Magazine* in February 1893
Main Characters: Grant Munro, Effie Munro, Lucy Hebron

Grant Munro asks Holmes for advice in connection with his wife, Effie. Her previous husband and her child had died of yellow fever in America, before Munro met her in England. They now live in the coun-

try near Norbury, and Effie had recently asked for some of her own money to be returned to her without any explanation. Munro had seen a livid-yellow face at the window of a recently rented neighbouring cottage, and soon afterwards noticed his wife leaving the house in the middle of the night. He had confronted her but was persuaded not to enquire further, but a few days later he had returned home early to find her absent. In the nearby cottage he found a photograph of his wife.

Holmes suspects blackmail and joins Munro in visiting the cottage. They find Effie there with the livid-faced girl seen at the window. The girl is Effie's daughter wearing a mask. Effie's first husband had been a negro and she had feared telling Munro about this. Munro accept the child as theirs, and the family returns home. Holmes is suitably chastened by his incorrect deductions.

Again there is no crime committed in this case, and Holmes asks Watson to mention the word "Norbury" if he ever again becomes over-confident. He can certainly be accused of ignoring his own advice not to make judgements without data, as he has very little relevant information when he expresses his first opinion. No explanation is given in the narrative for the fact that Effie repeatedly calls Grant "Jack". It has also been pointed out that the laws of Georgia would not have allowed the marriage of Effie and Hebron, but there is more than one Atlanta in America.

" 'TELL ME EVERYTHING,' I SAID." *Grant Munro becoming frustrated at his wife's lack of communication (above).*

"THERE WAS A LITTLE COAL-BLACK NEGRESS." *Holmes reveals to Grant and Watson the innocent face behind the mask (below).*

THE ADVENTURE OF THE STOCK-BROKER'S CLERK

First published: *The Strand Magazine* in March 1893
Main Characters: Hall Pycroft, Arthur Pinner, Harry Pinner, Mr Harris, Mr Price

Holmes's client, Hall Pycroft, travels with Holmes and Watson to Birmingham and outlines his case. He had been offered employment as a clerk at the London stock-broking firm of Mawson & Williams. He had then been offered better wages and prospects, complete with an advance of salary, with a new firm, the Franco-Midland Hardware Company, by an Arthur Pinner. He had been persuaded not to contact Mawson & Williams because they had apparently been insulting about him. Pycroft had met Arthur's brother, Harry, in Birmingham and been given the task of copying out lists of French businesses. Pycroft had suddenly realized that Arthur and Harry were the same man, and had called in Holmes.

On reaching Birmingham, Holmes and Watson are introduced to Pinner as Harris and Price, two gentlemen seeking employment. Pinner attempts to hang himself after reading in the newspaper that his real brother, Beddington – who had been passing as Pycroft at Mawson & Williams – had been arrested as he was leaving the building, having murdered a watchman whilst robbing the firm.

Holmes actually performs little in the way of deduction in this case as the events merely unfold around him. He does appreciate that Pycroft has been decoyed away from the scene of a proposed crime, and one might initially think that Holmes had the example of *The Red-Headed League* to prompt this. The internal chronologies of these two cases, however, reveal that this case preceded the one which had earlier been recorded by Watson.

THE ADVENTURE OF THE *"GLORIA SCOTT"*

First published: *The Strand Magazine* in April 1893
Main Characters: Victor Trevor, Mr Trevor, Hudson, Beddoes, James Armitage, Evans, Jack Prendergast

Holmes relates his earliest case to Watson, and recalls that at college he had been bitten by the dog of a fellow student, Victor Trevor, who had subsequently invited Holmes home to Donnithorpe in Norfolk. An elderly seaman called Hudson had arrived unannounced and made himself insultingly at home, indicating that he had some blackmailing power over Trevor Senior. Victor is eventually forced to castigate Hudson, who leaves, muttering threats, to visit a Mr Beddoes in Hampshire. When a cryptic note arrived from Hampshire, Trevor Senior suffered a stroke and later died. His papers revealed that, as James Armitage, he had been sentenced to transportation 30 years earlier, and that he had met two fellow convicts, Evans and Prendergast, on board the convict ship *Gloria Scott*. During a mutiny the ship was blown up but Armitage, Evans and Hudson, amongst others, survived. Evans and Armitage went on to make their fortunes in Australia before returning to England as Trevor and Beddoes. After the warning note was sent, neither Beddoes nor Hudson was heard of again.

In this case Holmes does little more than deduce information about Trevor Senior and decipher a coded note. It does supply some clues about Holmes's age, since he was at college in 1885, and some tantalizingly contradictory suggestions about where that college was located, connected with the keeping of dogs and whether Holmes was walking to chapel from the college or from the town when he was bitten.

THE ADVENTURE OF THE MUSGRAVE RITUAL

First published: *The Strand Magazine* in May 1893
Main Characters: Reginald Musgrave, Brunton, Rachel

Holmes recounts to Watson another early case, where his former college acquaintance, Reginald Musgrave, had reported problems with his butler, Brunton, a well-educated man who was over-fond of affairs with the female servants. Musgrave had dismissed Brunton after finding him looking through private family papers, including the seemingly meaningless Musgrave Ritual recited on inheriting the estate. Brunston had then disappeared, as had Rachel, a maid recently jilted by the butler. The lake had been dragged, but only a strange collection of objects had been found in a bag.

Holmes determines that the ritual contains directions, which he follows, to discover Brunton's body under a floor. Brunton had also followed the directions, found a treasure, then been trapped in the vault by

Rachel, who had then thrown the treasure into the lake before fleeing. The treasure proved to include the corroded ancient crown of England, entrusted to the Musgraves by Charles I before he was executed.

This is another unusual case, in that Watson does not take part in the proceedings. Musgrave takes his place to some extent, but he is not an entirely suitable replacement, being aristocratically remote, and, like all the Musgraves, lacking the intelligence to realize the significance of the ritual as Brunton had done. The fact that such an aristocrat would automatically attend Oxford or Cambridge, albeit without any requirements for scholarly abilities at that time, is used to suggest that Holmes, who was a college acquaintance, must also have attended one of these two universities.

THE ADVENTURE OF THE REIGATE SQUIRES

First published: *The Strand Magazine* in June 1893. First published as *The Adventure of the Reigate Squire* in England, and as *The Reigate Puzzle* in USA
Main Characters: Colonel Hayter, William Kirwan, Mr Cunningham, Alec Cunningham

Watson invites Holmes to recover from overwork at the home of his friend, Colonel Hayter, near Reigate. There they hear of a burglary at the Actons' house in which some peculiar items are taken. The next day they

THE PIECE OF THE NOTE FOUND IN THE DEAD MAN'S HAND. *To solve this case Holmes applied his elementary graphological skills.*

hear that a coachman, William Kirwan, has been murdered during a burglary at the Cunninghams' house, the fleeing murderer having been seen by Mr Cunningham and his son, Alec. The corner of a note was found in Kirwan's hand, mentioning an appointment. Holmes writes out a reward note, which Mr Cunningham has to correct, then, whilst examining the house, Holmes disappears. Watson then hears Holmes cry for help and, along with the Colonel and the Inspector, rushes to the landing to find Holmes being attacked by the Cunninghams. On being rescued Holmes produces the letter from which a corner had been torn. He had noticed that the words on the torn corner had been written alternately by two people, and had assumed that the peculiar objects stolen from the Actons' house had been taken to detract attention from the real purpose of the burglary, which was to obtain an important document involved in a land dispute. Holmes had disappeared to search for the torn note in the Cunninghams' rooms, having become suspicious when he realized that they could not have seen a fleeing murderer from their rooms as they had claimed. Kirwan had been killed because he had followed his masters when they burgled the Actons' house and attempted to blackmail them.

Holmes is rather cruel to Watson in this case, when he upsets a bowl of fruit and blames Watson for it, in order to distract attention whilst he disappears. It also has the distinction of involving a colonel who is neither a villain nor extremely rude. The copies of the letter which appear in the published versions do not include all the graphological details described by Holmes, which suggests that the original must have been lost.

CONAN DOYLE CHARACTERS

DR. WATSON

THE ADVENTURE OF THE CROOKED MAN

First published: *The Strand Magazine* in July 1893
Main Characters: Colonel Barclay, Mrs Barclay, Miss Morrison, Henry Wood,
Teddy the mongoose

Holmes informs Watson that he is investigating the murder in Aldershot of Colonel Barclay, who had risen from the ranks to command the Mallows. Mrs Barclay had returned home and had a row with her husband. After hearing a scream, the servants found the living room door locked on the inside, and on entering through the French window, found the Colonel dead and Mrs Barclay unconscious. The key to the door could not be found, but a club was lying near the Colonel and Mrs Barclay is suspected of murder.

On examining the house next day, Holmes finds the prints of a man and a strange creature which had run up the curtains. He deduces that the Colonel had either been killed by this man, who must have taken the door key, or died from hitting his head after fainting from seeing this man. Mrs Barclay's friend, Miss Morrison, mentions that they had seen a badly deformed man the night before, who had been well known to Mrs Barclay. Holmes interviews this man, Henry Wood, who had been a corporal in India when Barclay had been a sergeant and a rival for the future Mrs Barclay's hand. During a siege, Wood had been sent for help by Barclay, then was betrayed by him. He had become a prisoner

and was ill-treated until deformed, but had eventually escaped and returned to England. On meeting Mrs Barclay he had informed her of his fate and she had confronted the Colonel. When Wood arrived in the room the Colonel had died of shock. The strange animal was Wood's pet mongoose. Wood does not have to give evidence, as Mrs Barclay is cleared when the postmortem reveals that the Colonel died of apoplexy.

Some texts change the Mallows to the Munsters. The latter was a real regiment the history of which does not fit that of Colonel Barclay's regiment. Watson, as an old soldier, no doubt invented the former to protect the name of the actual regiment involved. The knowledge of the Bible exhibited by Holmes does not coincide with his normal attitude towards religion, but it may have been the dogmatic teaching of such biblical knowledge which originally drove him towards his rationalistic attitudes.

THE ADVENTURE OF THE RESIDENT PATIENT

First published: *The Strand Magazine* in August 1893
Main Characters: Dr Percy Trevelyan, Mr Blessington, Sutton, the Whittington bank gang

CONAN DOYLE CHARACTERS

PROFESSOR MORIARTY

Dr Percy Trevelyan informs Holmes that a wealthy patient, Mr Blessington, had established him in a good practice in Blessington's house, partly in exchange for the treatment of Blessington's heart condition. Blessington had recently become inexplicably agitated and increased the house security. Not long after, Trevelyan had been examining a visiting Russian nobleman who was accompanied by his son. The Russian had gone into a trance during the examination and Trevelyan left the room to obtain medicines. When he returned the Russians had gone. Blessington then found signs of intruders in his bedroom.

Holmes questions Blessington, but the latter is evasive. The next morning Blessington is found hanged in his bedroom, and Holmes deduces that the supposed Russians were responsible. Blessington, or Sutton as his real name was, had been a member of the Whittington bank gang. Years earlier Blessington had informed on the gang and became anxious on reading of their recent release from prison. Meanwhile, the gang members escape London, but are then believed to be lost at sea.

This case temporarily contained the mind-reading episode from *The Cardboard Box*, but the seasons described in the initial paragraph became confused. This version can still be found in some texts. Holmes can be accused himself for unjustly accusing the page at Blessington's house before he knows that the page has run away, since it is seemingly only the flight which would suggest guilt. However, Holmes does not always give all the indications of guilt which he has seen.

THE ADVENTURE OF THE GREEK INTERPRETER

First published: *The Strand Magazine* in September 1893
Main Characters: Mycroft Holmes, Mr Melas, Harold Latimer, William Kemp,
Paul Kratides, Sophy Kratides, Inspector Gregson

Watson is introduced for the first time to Holmes's brother, Mycroft. Mr Melas, Mycroft's neighbour, reports that he had recently been taken by Harold Latimer in a closed carriage to a country house to interpret for a Greek gentleman. He had found the gentleman guarded and gagged, able to communicate only in writing. He surreptitiously discovered that the man was Paul Kratides from Athens, and that he was being forcibly restrained. A woman called Sophy unexpectedly entered the room and recognized Kratides, but Melas was then rushed back to London, after being well paid. Mycroft had advertised for information and received Sophy's address, which is in Beckenham. Meanwhile Melas had been taken to question Kratides further.

Holmes, Watson and Mycroft collect Inspector Gregson and travel to Beckenham, where they find Melas unconscious and Kratides dead from noxious fumes. The latter had been trying to rescue his sister, Sophy, from the influence of Latimer and his colleague, William Kemp, but had been captured by them. They were attempting to force him to sign away rights to his and Sophy's property, and when they failed they had left Kratides and Melas to die as they fled with Sophy. News is later received of the death of the two men under mysterious circumstances in Buda-Pesth.

This case is remarkable for the introduction of the man who has superior deductive powers to those of Holmes, his brother

Mycroft. It is strange that Holmes has never mentioned him before, and even here Holmes does not reveal his actual importance. One is also left to wonder who the mysterious J. Davenport was, who informed Mycroft of Sophy's whereabouts. It is indicated in this case that Holmes may not always have been consistent in his attitudes to knowledge, for he had considered that astronomy was of no use to his profession in *A Study in Scarlet*, but he is able to discuss some rather technical aspects of astronomy in this case. Perhaps he had been involved in a case more recently which required such knowledge.

THE ADVENTURE OF THE NAVAL TREATY

First published: *The Strand Magazine* in November 1893
Main Characters: Percy Phelps, Annie Harrison, Joseph Harrison, Lord Holdhurst

Watson requests Holmes's assistance on behalf of an old school friend, Percy Phelps. At Phelps's house they meet Annie, his fiancée, who has been nursing him. He has suffered brain fever since losing an important naval treaty which he was copying alone in his office at the Foreign Office some ten weeks previously. He had visited the commissionaire's office and while there heard the bell ring from his own office. When he returned to his office the treaty was gone.

Holmes visits Lord Holdhurst, the Foreign Secretary and uncle of Phelps, and deduces that the theft must have been unplanned, since no-one knew that the treaty would be in Phelps's office. Holmes discovers the next day that there has been an attempted burglary in Phelps's sickroom, on the first night that Phelps had slept alone. He pretends to return to London with Phelps and Watson. Actually he returns to 221B the next morning, when Phelps is allowed to discover the missing treaty under a dish cover.

Holmes had caught Annie's brother, Joseph, attempting to recover the treaty from Phelps's sickroom. Joseph had visited Phelps unexpectedly and saw the treaty. He had stolen it to pay debts, and had hidden it in the room in which Phelps had since been sleeping. Although Holmes informs the police about the crime, he allows Harrison time to escape, to avoid scandal in the newspapers.

Holmes has, quite rightly, received a great deal of criticism over an incidental scene which is irrelevant to his analysis of the case. Holmes, in a pensive mood, remarks that the colour and scent of a rose are arbitrary and thus indicate some divine providence. These attributes of a rose are, of course, not pointless, since they attract insects to pollinate the flower. This temporary diversion from Holmes's rationalistic philosophy, however, reveals something of the complexity of his character which he normally strives to conceal.

"WHAT A LOVELY THING A ROSE IS." *Holmes in a rare moment of sentimental philosophizing (above).*

"HOLMES WAS WORKING HARD OVER A CHEMICAL INVESTIGATION." *Watson requests Holmes's expertise in helping an old school chum who has lost a treaty (left).*

THE ADVENTURE OF THE FINAL PROBLEM

First published: *The Strand Magazine* in December 1893
Main Character: Professor Moriarty

"PROFESSOR MORIARTY STOOD BEFORE ME." *The Napoleon of crime (above).*

"THE DEATH OF SHERLOCK HOLMES." *Watson imagines the final struggle that led to the mightly fall of Holmes and Moriarty (far right).*

"A SMALL SQUARE OF PAPER FLUTTERED DOWN." *Watson discovers Holmes's "final" letter to him (right).*

Watson attempts to correct rumours about the events which led to the disappearance of Holmes some years previously. Holmes had collected evidence which would lead to the arrest of the Moriarty gang, and to the execution of their leader, "The Napoleon of Crime". Holmes had been threatened by Moriarty and attacked by his agents. He asked Watson to accompany him on a trip to the Continent until the gang has been captured. Moriarty hired a special train to follow the pair, but they evaded him by leaving their Dover boat train and diverting to the Newhaven ferry.

On the Continent they learn that Moriarty had avoided arrest, and they continued their journey to reach Meiringen in Switzerland. Whilst walking near the Reichenbach Falls, Watson was decoyed back to their hotel, and returned to the Falls to find a note from Holmes which explained that Holmes and Moriarty were about to engage in a fight to the death. The signs of the struggle indicated that both men had

plunged over the Falls to their deaths, and Watson returned to England alone.

Conan Doyle intended this to be the very last Holmes story, and it neatly sums up Holmes's dedication to improving his world through the destruction of its worst criminal member. Holmes's ending could hardly be more dramatic, and yet the action is only surmised. The description poignantly reveals Watson's deepest feelings for Holmes and creates a great sense of loss. There are, however, some interesting problems left by the narrative. Watson claims that he has never heard of Moriarty, yet he was very familiar with him only a few years earlier in *The Valley of Fear*. There is also the strange reference to Holmes's fear of air-guns, which is not explained in any way.

THE HOUND OF THE BASKERVILLES

First published: *The Strand Magazine* from August 1901 to April 1902
Main Characters: Dr Mortimer, Sir Charles Baskerville, Sir Henry Baskerville, Barrymore, Jack Stapleton, Beryl Stapleton, Mr Frankland, Laura Lyons, Inspector Lestrade, the hound

Doctor Mortimer arrives at Baker Street to inform Holmes and Watson that Sir Charles Baskerville has died of heart failure in mysterious circumstances in the grounds of his Dartmoor home. Mortimer relates the legend of a spectral hound haunting the Baskerville family and he then asks for advice about the next heir, Sir Henry, who is about to arrive from Canada to take up his inheritance. On arrival, Sir Henry receives a cryptic note warning him away from the Moor. At his hotel one of his old boots is stolen.

Holmes sends Watson to accompany Sir Henry to Dartmoor with Doctor Mortimer, and there they find that a convicted murderer, Selden, has escaped from the prison on the Moor. Sir Henry meets a local butterfly collector, Jack Stapleton, and soon falls in love with Stapleton's sister, Beryl. Sir Henry's butler, Barrymore, is found signalling at night to the convict, and it is revealed that he has been supplying Selden with food because the latter is Barrymore's brother-in-law. Whilst vainly pursuing Selden with Sir Henry, Watson briefly sees a mysterious man standing on one of the Moor's tors.

Barrymore informs Watson that immediately prior to his death, Sir Charles had received a letter from a lady with the initials "LL", asking him to meet her at the gate to the Moor on the night he died. Barrymore also reports that Selden has seen the other man on the Moor. Watson discovers that the lady is Laura Lyons, and he interviews her but finds out little more.

Watson sets out onto the Moor to find the hiding place of "the man on the tor" only to

"HOLDING IT ONLY AN INCH OR TWO FROM HIS EYES." *Holmes examines the letter warning Sir Henry away from the Moor (above).*

"HOUND of the BASKERVILLES"
By Sir A. Conan Doyle.

POPULAR NOVELS ILLUSTRATED

EDWARDIAN POSTCARD (*far left*) *promoting* The Hound of the Baskervilles.

"OVER THE ROCKS WAS THRUST OUT AN EVIL YELLOW FACE." *Watson and Sir Henry disturb the escaped convict on the Moor (left).*

PETER CUSHING AND HIS PIPE
*(top and above). The pipe
used by the actor in the
Hammer Films production of*
The Hound of the
Baskervilles, *1959.*

discover that it is Holmes, who has been carrying out his own investigations. He has discovered that the murderer is Stapleton, who is married to his "sister" Beryl, and who has promised marriage to Laura Lyons, primarily to gain her assistance in decoying Sir Charles. As darkness falls they hear the cries of someone being pursued by a hound and find a body which appears to be that of Sir Henry. It is actually Selden, who is wearing some of Sir Henry's old clothes. Stapleton soon arrives on the scene, and Holmes informs him that he and Watson have been unsuccessful in their investigations and are to return to London. Holmes and Watson proceed to Baskerville Hall, where Holmes recognizes the likeness of Stapleton in the family portraits and realizes that he is the son of Sir Charles's

younger brother who had died, supposedly without issue, in South America. Holmes then persuades Sir Henry to join Stapleton for dinner on the next evening, and to walk back across the Moor to Baskerville Hall.

Holmes and Watson pretend to leave for London, but collect Lestrade from the station before hiding on the Moor outside Stapleton's house. Sir Henry leaves the house and vanishes into the mist just as the hound appears, chasing after Sir Henry. Holmes shoots the dog and discovers that its spectral appearance is due to the effect of phosphorescent paint. Beryl is found tied up in the house and Stapleton disappears into the mist on Grimpen Mire, where he is assumed to have drowned. Sir Henry sets off on a world trip to recover from his attack.

Holmes informs Watson that he had solved the outlines of the crime from deducing that an old boot had been taken in order to provide the hound with a scent, and that the warning note had come from a woman because of the perfume on it. He had traced most of Stapleton's history from the latter's careless revelation to Watson that he had once been a schoolteacher. The rest of the case had merely involved the confirmation of details.

" 'WHO–WHO'S THIS?' HE STAMMERED." *Stapleton, expecting to find the body of Sir Henry, finds Selden, the escaped convict, (opposite above right).*

BASIL RATHBONE AND NIGEL BRUCE *in a publicity still for Hollywood's* The Hound of the Baskervilles, *1939.*

This narrative was written after the loss of Holmes at Reichenbach, but deals with an earlier case. It is deservedly the most popular of all the Sherlock Holmes stories, and it contains few major problems, considering the length and complexity of the plot. It does contain some supreme examples of the annoying way in which Holmes prevents Watson, and thereby us, from being able to solve the case, in that he deliberately withholds such information as the faint perfume on the warning note. In addition we

"I SAW THE FIGURE OF A MAN UPON THE TOR." *Despite the bright moonlight Watson is unable to recognize the distinctive figure of his colleague Holmes (far left).*

"THE HOUND OF THE BASKERVILLES." *Not what one would classify as Man's Best Friend (left).*

THE CURSE OF THE
BASKERVILLES. *Francis de
Wolff as Dr Mortimer relates
the legend of the Baskerville
hound to Andre Morell and
Peter Cushing in the 1959
Hammer production.*

"HOLMES EMPTIED FIVE
BARRELS OF HIS REVOLVER
INTO THE CREATURE'S FLANK."
*Holmes saves Sir Henry from
the jaws of death and ends the
danger of the phosphorescent
hound.*

are not made suspicious of Stapleton, in
that we are not made privy to the investigations which Holmes carries out into his
background. Perhaps the main difficulty in
the plot is the one which Holmes himself
does not adequately answer, which is exactly how Stapleton intended taking possession
of the estate if his plan to murder Sir Henry
had been successful. A solution might in-
volve the use of an agent to claim the estate,
as Holmes suggests, with the later removal
of that agent, in the same way that Beryl
and Laura might have required "removal".
One rather unsatisfactory element of the
narrative is the way that Sir Henry appears
to abandon his love for Beryl, when the
latter had done everything she could to
help him short of directly betraying her
husband. These minor points are more
than compensated for by the totally dramatic effect of the narrative. There can be few
who do not still feel a sense of excitement
when they read such lines as "Mr Holmes,
they were the footprints of a gigantic
hound!"

THE ADVENTURE OF THE EMPTY HOUSE

First published: *Collier's* in September 1903
Main Characters: Colonel Moran, Ronald Adair, Inspector Lestrade

Watson visits the scene of the murder of Ronald Adair, who has been shot with a bullet from a short-range revolver, in a room locked from the inside. Watson is followed home by an elderly bookseller, who dramatically reveals himself to be Holmes. Holmes explains that he defeated Moriarty three years previously and then climbed a cliff to leave no traces of his escape, although he was seen doing this by Colonel Moran, Moriarty's chief assistant. Holmes has travelled the world, and on returning has become involved in the "Park Lane mystery".

That night, Holmes takes Watson to an empty house opposite 221B, from which they see the silhouette of a bust of Holmes projected onto the curtain of their old flat. Moran enters the empty house and shoots the bust of Holmes with a powerful air-gun, firing a revolver bullet across the street. After arresting Moran, Holmes explains to

Lestrade that Moran had killed Adair in the same way.

This narrative presents many difficulties. Holmes states that he disappeared to confound remaining members of the Moriarty gang, yet Moran was already aware of his survival. Holmes's journey to Tibet would have been almost impossible in those days, and it certainly confused Watson who records in the *Strand* version that Holmes visited the Head Llama, rather than the Head Lama! Also, Holmes could not have visited the Khalifa in Khartoum at that time since the Khalifa left that city in 1885. Perhaps Holmes was engaged in activities which Mycroft would not allow him to reveal even to Watson. The reference to air-guns in *The Final Problem* would have been an excellent link to *The Empty House*, but one must recall that *The Final Problem* had been written as the last Holmes case. In *The Empty House* we discover that both Professor Moriarty and his brother, Colonel Moriarty, have the name of James. This may have been part of their surname, and it is therefore a pity that we are not given the full name of the third Moriarty brother. In spite of its many problems, the case is redeemed by the return of Holmes!

VIEWS OF THE DRAWING ROOM AT 221B *(above and left). The reconstructed room is in the Sherlock Holmes Pub in London.*

"I CREPT FORWARD AND LOOKED ACROSS AT THE FAMILIAR WINDOW." *Standing next to the detective Watson is amazed at the silhouette of Holmes illuminated in the drawing room of 221B across the street.*

THE ADVENTURE OF THE NORWOOD BUILDER

First published: *Collier's* in October 1903
Main Characters: John McFarlane, Jonas Oldacre, Inspector Lestrade

John Hector McFarlane visits 221B hurriedly and informs Holmes that he is about to be arrested for the murder of Jonas Oldacre, immediately before Lestrade arrives to do just that. Oldacre, a builder living in Norwood, had disappeared and McFarlane's bloody walking stick had been found at his home, together with some bones in the ashes of a fire. McFarlane claims that he had been asked to finalize Oldacre's will and had found that Oldacre was leaving everything to him. Oldacre had explained that he had known McFarlane's parents, but that he had no relatives of his own to leave his estate to, and had asked

COLLIER'S THE NORWOOD BUILDER. American illustrator Frederic Dorr Steele's rendition of Holmes. The handprint on the wall is artistic licence. Oldacre used McFarlane's thumb print according to Watson.

McFarlane to visit his house late at night to complete the matter. Holmes discovers that, when young, Oldacre had been rejected as a suitor by McFarlane's mother, and that there are no valuable documents at the house. He also finds that large bank payments had been made recently by Oldacre to a Mr Cornelius.

On being summoned to Oldacre's house by Lestrade to examine a bloody thumb print which is McFarlane's, Holmes informs Watson that it had not been there the day before, yet McFarlane is still in gaol. Holmes then starts a smoky fire in the house, which drives Oldacre out of the hiding place which Holmes had discovered by comparing the internal and external dimensions of the house. McFarlane's print had been obtained by Oldacre from a wax seal, and he had planned the whole affair out of revenge against Mrs McFarlane.

This case sees the introduction of the use of fingerprints as evidence, although it is interesting that this particular thumb print is a false one. We also discover something of the value which Holmes attached to Watson's assistance in the way that he has indirectly bought Watson's practice. Since Holmes was not in favour of publicity, it can be suggested that Watson may well have provided assistance for Holmes which his own modesty prevented him from mentioning, or that he did not wish to diminish the image of Holmes which he was largely responsible for having created.

THE ADVENTURE OF THE DANCING MEN

First published: *The Strand Magazine* in December 1903
Main Characters: Hilton Cubitt, Elsie Cubitt, Abe Slaney

Mr Hilton Cubitt gives Holmes a copy of a series of chalked stickmen figures which had been appearing at his house in Norfolk, and asks him to decipher them. Cubitt had

married Elsie Patrick, an American, who had asked him not to enquire into her past, and she had fainted when shown the first of the figures. Holmes analyses the figures but is unable to travel immediately to Norfolk. He eventually arrives to find that Cubitt and his wife have been shot. The servants had heard a loud explosion from the study, followed by a lesser one, and found Cubitt dead and his wife wounded, with a pistol containing two empty chambers. Holmes finds a third bullet embedded in the edge of a window, with the empty case outside.

Holmes then sends a note to a nearby farm, and explains that the figures are an alphabetical substitution code which he had solved by letter-frequency analysis. His note, using this code, had invited the originator of the messages, Abe Slaney, to visit Elsie. Slaney is arrested on arrival and confesses that he had been a member of a gang run by Elsie's father, the inventor of the code. He had been engaged to her, but she had left America when he would not give up crime. Slaney had met Elsie in the study and been surprised by Cubitt. They had exchanged shots, Slaney's causing Cubitt's fatal wound, and this had been heard as one loud explosion. Elsie had attempted suicide, causing the second explosion, but she later recovers. Holmes had deduced most of this from the amount of gun smoke which had been noted in the study.

This is another of Holmes's unsatisfactory cases, since he loses his client through being unable to travel to Norfolk overnight. In spite of the possibility of hiring special trains, this is a reminder that overnight, or even late-night, trains were not very common in England during the age of Victoria. The code used in this case is an extremely simple one, and it is therefore unfortunate that those who attempt to emulate Holmes's breaking of the code will find it rather difficult to do so, for most versions of the case have mistakes introduced by the printers, and these mistakes vary according to the printer. The fact that Holmes was keeping Watson's cheque book is possibly a reminder that Watson was inclined to spend too much of his pension on horseracing.

"HOLMES CLAPPED A PISTOL TO HIS HEAD AND MARTIN SLIPPED THE HANDCUFFS OVER HIS WRISTS." *The sleuth traps the not-so-honest Abe.*

THE DANCING MEN. *Part of the uncompleted message. Deciphered, it reads: "at Elri".*

THE ADVENTURE OF THE SOLITARY CYCLIST

First published: *Collier's* in December 1903
Main Characters: Violet Smith, Bob Carruthers, Jack Woodley, Mr Williamson

"AS WE APPROACHED, THE LADY STAGGERED AGAINST THE TRUNK OF THE TREE." *Rescued from an unsavoury marriage.*

"HOLMES TOSSED THE END OF HIS CIGARETTE INTO THE GRATE." *Perhaps an ashtray was too much to ask (below).*

Violet Smith informs Holmes that in response to a newspaper advertisement she and her mother had contacted a Mr Carruthers and a Mr Woodley, who told them that their last relative, Violet's uncle, had died penniless in South Africa, but that he had asked them to care for his relatives. Carruthers offers Violet employment, living at his home near Farnham. At the house, Woodley had attempted to force his attentions on Violet and had been forcibly ejected by Carruthers. As Violet cycled to the station each weekend after this she noted that she was being followed by a bearded cyclist.

Watson investigates and sees a cyclist vanish into the grounds of a house rented by a Mr Williamson. Holmes discovers that Williamson is possibly a defrocked priest. Carruthers proposes to Violet, which prompts her decision to leave. Holmes and Watson

travel to meet her and are joined by the bearded cyclist, who turns out to be Carruthers, then find that she has just been forcibly "married" by Williamson (an unfrocked priest) to Woodley. Carruthers shoots Woodley and wounds him.

It is revealed that Carruthers and Woodley knew that Violet's uncle was rich and about to die, and they had sought out his only two relatives: Woodley won at cards the "right" to marry Violet, but Carruthers fell in love with her and tried to protect her. Woodley and Williamson are imprisoned.

There is some confusion as to who the solitary cyclist is. Since Violet is the most important cyclist it might be thought to be her, and Watson's introduction appears to indicate this, but Carruthers is specifically referred to as a solitary cyclist later in the case. It would be very difficult to explain why Woodley bothered obtaining a marriage licence, since the "wedding" is illegal on several other grounds. The editor of *The Strand Magazine* rejected the first draft of this case because Holmes did not appear to have had enough to do, which may account for Watson recording Holmes's criticisms of himself so strongly.

THE ADVENTURE OF THE PRIORY SCHOOL

First published: *Collier's* in January 1904
Main Characters: Dr Thorneycroft Huxtable, the Duke of Holdernesse, Lord Saltire, Heidegger, James Wilder, Reuben Hayes

Dr Huxtable, the headmaster of the Priory School, explains that Lord Saltire, the son of the Duke of Holdernesse, has disappeared from his school in the Peak District. A German master, Heidegger, is also missing. Holmes and Watson return with Huxtable to the school. The Duke's secretary, James Wilder, rebukes Huxtable for involving outside assistance, but then the Duke reluctantly asks for Holmes's help. Following bicycle tracks amongst the cow tracks on the moors, Holmes finds Heidegger's body, and then continues to the Fighting Cock inn, where the owner, Reuben Hayes, although uncooperative, reveals that he had once been dismissed from the service of the Duke.

After realizing that he had seen no cows on the moors, Holmes deduces that Lord Saltire must have been abducted using a horse with cowprint shoes, and he notices that Hayes's horses have new shoes. Leaving the inn, Holmes sees Wilder arrive there on a bicycle with the same tread as the one on the moors. Hayes then flees. Holmes confronts the Duke with knowing that his son has been abducted by Wilder, and the Duke reveals that Wilder is his illegitimate son. Holmes announces that he has arranged the arrest of Hayes, and Lord Saltire is retrieved from the inn. The Duke states that Wilder will leave for Australia. Holmes permits this, even though Wilder is the instigator of the kidnapping of Lord Saltire and the murder of Heidegger by Hayes on the moors.

There is some discussion as to whether the Duke attempts to bribe Holmes, and whether the latter actually accepts such an offer, for the reward appears to double. Watson's Literary Agent had to admit some incorrect interference in the narrative, when he discovered that one cannot determine the direction of travel of a bicycle in the way described. Holmes obviously used other signs to assist his deduction, but, as often happened, Watson possibly did not record all of them. This case involves an extreme example of Holmes by-passing the due process of law without, however, his usual moral justification.

"I HEARD HIM CHUCKLE AS THE LIGHT FELL UPON A PATCHED DUNLOP TYRE." *Holmes begins to deflate the murder mystery (far left).*

"THERE LAY THE UNFORTUNATE RIDER." *Holmes and Watson find the body of Heidegger.*

THE ADVENTURE OF BLACK PETER

First published: *Collier's* in February 1904
Main Characters: Inspector Hopkins, Peter Carey, John Neligan, Patrick Cairns

Holmes informs Watson that he has vainly spent the early morning attempting to pierce a pig's carcase with a harpoon. Inspector Hopkins relates that Captain "Black Peter" Carey, a retired whaler, had been found harpooned to the wall in his garden hut. On visiting the hut, Holmes, Watson and Hopkins find that someone has attempted to gain entry since the murder. When the intruder returns he is found to be John Hopley Neligan, the son of a banker who had failed in business, fled in a small yacht across the North Sea, then vanished. Some of the shares he had been carrying had recently come onto the market, and Neligan had traced them to Carey, and he claims that he was trying to discover more about his father from Carey's logbooks.

Hopkins arrests Neligan. Holmes advertises for a harpooner, and when a Patrick Cairns visits Holmes for the job he is arrested by Holmes. Neligan senior had been rescued by Carey's boat, but Cairns had seen Carey throw Neligan into the sea after robbing him of the shares he was carrying. Cairns had visited Carey and killed him during a quarrel over sharing the ill-gotten gains. Holmes had deduced that the killer was a harpooner from a sealskin pouch found in the hut, from the rum on a table, and from the strength and skill needed to pierce a man with a harpoon.

Once again, this is a classic example of Holmes examining the relevant information where others cling to only the more obvious evidence. Hopkins is quite correct when he warns John Neligan that he should keep the rest of his statement for the courts, for police officials at that time were specifically ordered not to take statements from those who might be accused. This, of course, constantly places Holmes at an advantage over those officials who obey this particular regulation, although there are numerous examples of it being ignored.

THE ADVENTURE OF CHARLES AUGUSTUS MILVERTON

First published: *Collier's* in March 1904
Main Characters: Lady Eva Brackwell, Charles Augustus Milverton, Agatha, Inspector Lestrade

Holmes is asked by Lady Brackwell to retrieve some imprudent letters from Charles Augustus Milverton, an infamous blackmailer. Milverton refuses Holmes's offer of a reduced settlement, and Holmes then obtains information about Milverton's house by becoming engaged to Milverton's maid, Agatha. With Watson he burgles the house, but they have to hide when Milverton arrives to interview a maid who wishes to sell some letters. The "maid" is found to be a lady whose husband killed himself after Milverton revealed her indiscretions.

The lady shoots Milverton dead and flees. Holmes destroys the material in Milverton's safe before he and Watson narrowly escape. Lestrade asks Holmes for assistance but Holmes refuses on the grounds that some crimes deserve to go unpunished. Holmes later identifies the lady to Watson.

There are numerous moral problems in this case. Firstly Holmes and Watson commit the crime of burglary, then Holmes destroys private property from Milverton's safe. Holmes condones a murder, and refuses to help the police, even when he discovers who the murderer is. Even Watson threatens Holmes, indicating that he will report Holmes for burglary if he does not allow Watson to help. Perhaps Holmes's worst "crime", however, is the way in which he uses the maid, Agatha, to satisfy his own requirements. The case does contain an excellent example of Holmes's humour, though, when he points out to Inspector Lestrade that the description of one of the men seen leaving the scene of the murder fits that of Watson.

HUBERT WILLIS AND EILLE NORWOOD. *Norwood as Holmes shows Willis as Watson the key to the case in the 1922 film of* Charles Augustus Milverton.

"EXHIBITING THE BUTT OF A LARGE REVOLVER, WHICH PROJECTED FROM THE INSIDE POCKET." *Milverton makes his exit (above left).*

"THEN HE STAGGERED TO HIS FEET AND RECEIVED ANOTHER SHOT." *Milverton gets more than he blackmailed for (far left).*

"FOLLOWING HIS GAZE I SAW THE PICTURE OF A REGAL AND STATELY LADY IN COURT DRESS." *Holmes identifies the woman who ended the corrupt Milverton's life.*

THE ADVENTURE OF THE SIX NAPOLEONS

First published: *Collier's* in April 1904
Main Characters: Inspector Lestrade, Beppo, Pietro Venucci

Lestrade reports that some recent burglaries had resulted in the smashing of busts of Napoleon, but he calls for Holmes's assistance when a further smashing involves a murder. A photograph on the body of the dead man is found to be of Beppo, an art-work odd-job man who has recently completed a one-year sentence for knifing a fellow Italian. Holmes finds that the smashed busts are from a batch of six, made a year previously, and Lestrade discovers that the dead man was Pietro Venucci, an Italian assassin.

Holmes, Watson and Lestrade wait at a house where one of the two remaining busts is located and arrest a burglar who smashes the bust. Holmes then buys the last bust and smashes it to find the black pearl of the Borgias inside. Beppo had stuck the pearl in the still-wet bust at the manufacturers where he worked, prior to being arrested for the knifing. Venucci had possibly been connected with the original theft of the pearl and had been killed in a struggle when Beppo had obtained that particular bust.

Holmes appears to take a very serious risk in this case when he chooses which house to wait at for Beppo. He might at least have had Lestrade guard the other house. It is also difficult to explain why Holmes has the owner of the final bust sign all rights of possession to him, as neither of them has any right to the pearl. Perhaps Holmes did not want the owner to realize the real value of the bust, in terms of a possible reward.

THE ADVENTURE OF THE THREE STUDENTS

First published: *The Strand Magazine* in June 1904
Main Characters: Hilton Soames, Bannister, Gilchrist

Whilst carrying out some private researches at a university, Holmes is asked by Hilton Soames, a tutor, to investigate the compromising of a Greek examination paper. Soames had returned to his rooms to find a key in the door, the paper moved, some pencil sharpenings and a scratch on the writing desk. His servant, Bannister, had carelessly left the key in the door, and had almost fainted when shown the paper. Holmes sees that the room has very high-set windows, and finds some pellets of dark clay and sawdust in the room. He deduces that the intruder had been there for about a quarter of an hour.

There are three students living above the room who are suspect, and after investigating these and some locations in the town, Holmes accuses Bannister of finding the culprit and concealing him in Soames's bedroom until the coast was clear. One of the students, Gilchrist, is called and confesses. Holmes had deduced the culprit from his height, which had enabled him to see the paper through the high window, and that the pellets came from a long-jump pit, with the scratch being caused by Gilchrist's spiked shoes. Bannister had not almost fainted, but sat down to hide Gilchrist's gloves. Bannister had been butler to Gilchrist's father and wished to help him. Gilchrist had already decided not to take the examination, but to leave for service with the Rhodesian Police.

This is an extremely important case in connection with the discussion of Holmes's own university. It provides many clues but some of these are contradictory. Holmes is obviously familiar with this town, as opposed to the Cambridge of *The Missing Three-Quarter*. The expression "quadrangle" is used, which suggests Oxford, as opposed to the use of "court" at Cambridge. The black clay for jumping pits, however, is a mark of the Cambridge of that time. It has been pointed out that not only are the chapters in Thucydides too short for half a chapter to take so long to copy, but that a cheat would need only to note the beginning and the end of an extract from such a well-known work.

THE ADVENTURE OF THE GOLDEN PINCE-NEZ

First published: *The Strand Magazine* in July 1904
Main Characters: Inspector Hopkins, Professor Coram, Anna

Inspector Hopkins informs Holmes that he has been investigating the death of Professor Coram's secretary, Willoughby Smith. A scream had been heard and Smith was found bleeding from the neck; his last words were to tell the professor that " – it was she". No-one had been found, although all the exits from the house were blocked. In Smith's hand there was a pair of golden pince-nez. Holmes examines these and produces a detailed description of the owner, a lady. The next day Holmes visits the house and smokes several cigarettes in the bedroom where the professor spends almost all of his time. Holmes leaves the room, then on his return is able to reveal the owner of the pince-nez hiding in the room, having noted her foot marks in the cigarette ash which he had scattered.

The woman is Anna, a Russian Nihilist and Coram's estranged wife, whom he had betrayed in Russia. After her release she had travelled to England and had broken into Coram's house to obtain papers to free her lover back in Russia, when she was then discovered by Smith. They struggled, he grabbed her pince-nez and she stabbed Smith in the neck. Without her pince-nez Anna had accidentally run into Coram's room while trying to escape, and Coram had hidden Anna to prevent his past from being revealed. The secretary's last words

"THE BODY WAS FOUND NEAR THE BUREAU, AND JUST TO THE LEFT OF IT, AS MARKED UPON THAT CHART." *Inspector Hopkins shows Holmes where the body of the unfortunate secretary lay.*

were to warn Coram that the murderer was the lady he had reported seeing earlier that day. In desperation Anna takes poison and dies, but Holmes then takes the papers to the Russian Embassy on her behalf.

Anna's expectation that the papers she sought would be likely to result in the freeing of a Nihilist in Russia towards the end of the nineteenth century does not seem likely. Perhaps, however, Holmes would have been more successful, especially if he had similar connections with the royal house there that he seems to have had with most others. He must have seemed ill-mannered to Coram, for he not only rudely asked for more cigarettes but he also walked about flicking ash everywhere.

THE ADVENTURE OF THE MISSING THREE-QUARTER

First published: *The Strand Magazine* in August 1904
Main Characters: Cyril Overton, Godfrey Staunton, Lord Mount-James, Dr Leslie Armstrong, Pompey the dog

THE HOUND TAKES THE LEAD. *Holmes didn't always have trouble with dogs as Dorr Steele illustrated for his cover of* Collier's, *26th November 1904.*

THE ADVENTURE
of the
MISSING THREE-QUARTER

VOL XXXIV No 9   NOVEMBER 26   PRICE 10 CENTS

Cyril Overton, captain of the Cambridge University rugby team, informs Holmes that Godfrey Staunton, their wing three-quarter, and heir to Lord Mount-James, had received a note the previous evening then disappeared with the man who delivered it. At Staunton's hotel Holmes finds the last six words of a telegram written by Staunton, reversed on a blotter. Holmes discovers that the telegram was sent to a Dr Leslie Armstrong, but when he visits Armstrong in Cambridge he finds him evasive. Holmes follows Armstrong's carriage by bicycle, but is spotted and warned off. Holmes then sprays the wheels of Armstrong's carriage with aniseed and follows its scent using Pompey, a draghound.

At a country cottage Holmes and Watson find Godfrey Staunton and a dead lady. Armstrong confesses that Staunton had secretly married the lady, and that he had returned to her immediately when he had heard that she was dying. The marriage had been kept secret for fear that Lord Mount-James would disinherit Staunton.

This is yet another case in which no crime is committed and Holmes reveals great sensitivity when he finds that this is so. It is an important case in the determining of Holmes's university, wherein his reference to Cambridge as an "inhospitable town" and his lack of familiarity with the surrounding countryside suggest that he did not attend that university. It must be noted, however, that his "inhospitable" reference is used immediately after he and Watson are ejected from Armstrong's house, and Holmes may well not have been the sort of student who frequented the countryside surrounding his college.

THE ADVENTURE OF THE ABBEY GRANGE

First published: *The Strand Magazine* in September 1904
Main Characters: Inspector Hopkins, Sir Eustace Brackenstall, Lady Brackenstall, Jack Croker

Inspector Hopkins calls for Holmes's assistance over the murder of Sir Eustace Brackenstall, but regrets this call when Lady Brackenstall describes the murderers in a way that fits the Randall gang. She admits that her marriage had not been happy, as her husband was a brutal drunkard. She had been attacked by the robbers and tied to a chair; when her husband arrived he was killed with a poker.

Whilst returning to London, Holmes realizes that several points in Lady Brackenstall's account are incorrect. On further examining the room he finds that the bell-rope used to tie her up had been carefully cut, so as not to sound the bell, and that it had been tied in sailor's knots. There was also blood on the seat of the chair to which she was supposedly tied. Noticing a hole in the ice of the house's pond, Holmes suggests that Hopkins should check it, and the silver supposedly taken by the robbers is found there. The Randall gang is also found to have been elsewhere at the time of the crime. Holmes checks shipping registers and invites a Captain Croker to visit him.

Croker admits that he had known and loved Lady Brackenstall before her marriage, and, having heard of her husband's brutality, had met with her since. On Croker's last visit Sir Eustace had discovered the two lovers and attacked them, whereupon Croker killed him in self-defence. The "robbery" had been staged before Croker left. Holmes uses Watson as a jury and they find Croker not guilty.

This is the most blatant example of Holmes considering himself to be superior to the law, and his trial actually makes a mockery of the law, since by deciding that a real court of law would not deal with the case properly he has already prejudged the matter. There is, after all, no certainty that Croker's account is correct, for he could very easily have actually murdered Sir Eustace in cold blood. It is in this case, in response to Holmes's criticisms, that Watson urges Holmes to write his own account of his cases. Interestingly, when Holmes does this, in *The Blanched Soldier* and *The Lion's Mane*, his efforts are not noticeably different in style from those of Watson.

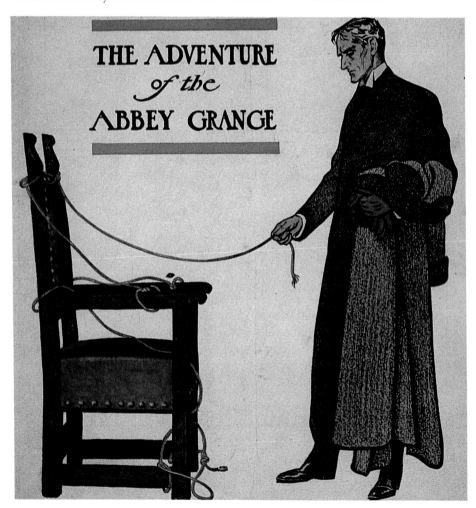

HOLMES UNTIES A SUSPICIOUS KNOT. *The sleuth decides that no wife should have to endure the sort of marriage Lady Brackenstall had found herself tied to. The Dorr Steele cover for* Collier's, *31st December 1904.*

THE ADVENTURE OF THE SECOND STAIN

First published: *The Strand Magazine* in December 1904
Main Characters: Lord Bellinger, Trelawney Hope, Eduardo Lucas/Henri Fournaye, Mme Fournaye, Lady Hilda Trelawney Hope, Inspector Lestrade

Lord Bellinger and the Right Honourable Trelawney Hope inform Holmes that a letter from a foreign potentate has been taken from Hope's home, and that its publication could cause a European war. Holmes then finds that a foreign agent, Eduardo Lucas, has been murdered. Lady Hilda Trelawney Hope then visits Holmes to enquire about the missing document, but Holmes will not divulge its nature. Lucas was apparently known as Henri Fournaye in France, and his wife is found in a deranged state of Paris. At Lucas's London house, Lestrade shows Holmes that the carpet on which Lucas's body was found had been turned round, as the stain on the carpet does not correspond with that on the floor. With Holmes's encouragement Lestrade discovers that a lady visitor had been left alone in the room after the murder.

Holmes visits Lady Hilda and forces her to return the document, which she had taken and given to Lucas because the latter was blackmailing her. Lady Hilda had seen Lucas hide the letter under the floor beneath the carpet, and then saw his wife kill him because she jealously assumed that Lady Hilda was Lucas's mistress. She retrieved the letter, carelessly leaving the carpet turned round, and replaced it in Hope's despatch box, where it is then thought to have been all the time, although Lord Bellinger suspects otherwise.

It is extraordinary that governmental officials should have kept such a potentially dangerous document once its contents were known by the few who needed to know them, but it is even more amazing that one of those officials should then take it home with him. This particular case is extremely difficult to date, but there are strong suggestions that Lord Bellinger is Gladstone: from the illustrations that appeared in *The Strand Magazine*, Sidney Paget certainly appears to have thought this.

THE ADVENTURE OF WISTERIA LODGE

First published: *Collier's* in August 1908. Published as *A Reminiscence of Mr Sherlock Holmes*
Main Characters: Scott Eccles, Inspector Gregson, Inspector Baynes, Aloysius Garcia, Mr Henderson/Don Murillo, Miss Burnett/Signora Victor Durando

Scott Eccles arrives at 221B, closely followed by Inspectors Gregson and Baynes who are investigating the death of Aloysius Garcia of Wisteria Lodge near Esher. A letter from Eccles had been found on the body. Eccles states that he had stayed with Garcia the previous night and that Garcia had visited his bedroom to see him at 1AM. Garcia, however, had apparently been murdered before then, at least a mile from the house. A note from a lady had also been found in the house, mentioning colour codings and rooms.

Holmes deduces that Garcia had intended using Eccles for an alibi by altering the clocks in the house. Holmes investigates the owners of large houses near Wisteria Lodge, and finds that one is a reclusive foreigner, Mr Henderson. He has two children and a governess, Miss Burnett, and Holmes surmises that the note came from her and that Garcia was travelling to the house when killed.

Shortly afterwards Miss Burnett is delivered to 221B by one of Holmes's agents; she had escaped from Henderson, who was himself fleeing. She reveals that Henderson is Don Murillo, the Tiger of San Pedro, a dictator who had recently escaped from a revolution in his country. Miss Burnett's real name is Signora Victor Durando, and her husband had been shot on Murillo's orders. Determined on revenge she had joined a group dedicated to the assassination of Murillo, which included Garcia. Signora Durando, as Miss Burnett, had managed to become Murillo's governess. She had written the note to inform Garcia where Murillo would be, but Murillo had intercepted the note and trapped Garcia. She had been drugged when Murillo was about to leave, but had escaped. Six months later, Murillo is killed in Spain.

Eccles must have been a very sound sleeper for Garcia to have changed the time on Eccles' watch, as surely he must have done in case Eccles checked what the real time was. Garcia also seems to have attempted to establish an alibi for the wrong time, for 1AM must have provided him with time to have returned from Murillo's house. One must also suggest that it was rather foolish of Murillo to have kept Signora Durando alive, for he can hardly have had anything to fear from killing her.

THE ADVENTURE OF THE BRUCE-PARTINGTON PLANS

First published: *The Strand Magazine* in December 1908
Main Characters: Arthur Cadogan West, Mycroft Holmes, Sir James Walker, Sidney Johnson, Colonel Valentine Walker, Herr Oberstein

"THERE WAS A FACE LOOKING IN AT ME THROUGH THE LOWER PANE." PC Walters begins to describe the unwelcome creature that had disturbed his reading. Illustrated by Arthur Twidle.

The body of Arthur Cadogan West, a junior clerk at the Admiralty, has been found beside an underground railway line. Mycroft informs Sherlock Holmes that some of the plans for the revolutionary Bruce-Partington submarine had been found on the body, and that others were still missing. The only two men who had keys to the plans were Sir James Walker and Sidney Johnson, and Holmes later finds that Sir James has died of shame over the loss. Holmes deduces that the body must have fallen from the top of a train as it swerved, and that it must have been placed on top at a point where the train had stopped. West's fiancée informs Holmes that she had been walking with West near the Admiralty on the night of the tragedy, when he had suddenly left her and dashed off into the fog. Holmes locates the house of a German spy whose window overlooks a point where trains temporarily stop.

Holmes, by pretending to be the spy, tempts the man who stole the plans into a rendezvous. The thief is found to be the brother of Sir James, Colonel Valentine Walker. He had taken impressions of his brother's keys for the spy, Herr Oberstein, to pay off debts. Oberstein is similarly lured to the house and the plans are recovered. Soon after this, Holmes visits Windsor, where he obtains an emerald tie-pin from "a certain gracious lady"!

This is one of the most political of the Holmes cases, with references to inter-national spying and the concealed diversion of governmental funds. It also shows an awareness of submarine developments, although these were at an early stage at that time, and the two Holmeses shared this interest with Watson's Literary Agent. It is rather strange that Mycroft has to produce a list of spies, since Sherlock was very famil-iar with them only a few years earlier in *The Second Stain* when his list included Ober-stein. It appears that international negotia-tions may have intruded in the sentencing of Oberstein, for he receives only fifteen years.

"HE SPRANG FORWARD WITH CLENCHED HANDS TOWARDS MY COMPANION." *Sterndale meets his match in Holmes.*

"WE LURCHED THROUGH THE DOOR, AND AN INSTANT AFTERWARDS HAD THROWN OURSELVES DOWN UPON THE GRASS PLOT." *The detectives escape the Devil's Foot poison. Illustrated by Gilbert Holiday.*

THE ADVENTURE OF THE DEVIL'S FOOT

First published: *The Strand Magazine* in December 1910
Main Characters: Mr Roundhay, Mortimer Tregennis, Owen Tregennis, Brenda Tregennis, Leon Sterndale

Ill health forces Holmes to rest in Cornwall with Watson, and there they are visited by the local vicar, Mr Roundhay, and his lod-ger, Mortimer Tregennis. The latter had left his two brothers Owen and George, and his sister Brenda, playing cards at their home the previous night. In the morning they had been found still at the table; the brothers demented and the sister dead. After examining the house Holmes is vis-ited by another local resident Leon Stern-dale, the famous explorer, who has can-celled a trip to Africa over the tragedy. Mortimer Tregennis then dies of the same symptoms as his sister.

Holmes finds some white powder on the top of a lamp, and when he burns some of this on an identical lamp, he and Watson are almost poisoned. Holmes deduces that Mortimer had caused the first poisonings, because of a family quarrel, but had then been poisoned himself by Sterndale when he discovered that Mortimer had taken the Devil's Foot poison from him. Sterndale had loved Brenda, and had thus returned to avenge her death. Holmes allows Stern-dale to leave for work in Africa.

A great deal of interest has been produced in this case with Watson's reference to Hol-mes's "occasional indiscretions", which had possibly aggravated his illness from over-work. There have been suggestions that this may indicate further drug abuse by Holmes at a later stage in his career. It may also have been a reference to Holmes's overuse of tobacco, since this is referred to on several occasions during the case and therefore seems to have been a preoccupation of Watson. Possibly this was the result of some new-fangled medical opinions which implied that smoking was connected with ill health!

" 'THE MOST EXTRAORDINARY AND TRAGIC AFFAIR HAS OCCURRED DURING THE NIGHT,' SAID THE VICAR." *Holmes and Watson have an unexpected visit from Mr Roundhay and Mr Mortimer Tregennis.*

THE ADVENTURE OF THE RED CIRCLE

First published: *The Strand Magazine* in March and April 1911
Main Characters: Mrs Warren, Mr Warren, Inspector Gregson, Mr Leverton,
Emilia Lucca, Gennaro Lucca, Giuseppe Gorgiano

Mrs Warren informs Holmes that she is concerned about a lodger who has not left his rooms for ten days. He leaves notes for requisites, which had included the *Daily Gazette*. Holmes examines back issues of this newspaper to discover a series of cryptic messages beginning when the lodger arrived. Mr Warren is abducted for a short time then released, and Holmes believes the abductors were after the lodger. He also believes that the lodger is not the person who booked the room, and confirms this when he sees a lady collect things left at the door of the rooms. He also sees a message being passed in code by candle from a window opposite the rooms, reading "beware, danger" in Italian.

Nearby Holmes then finds Inspector Gregson, who introduces Mr Leverton from Pinkerton's American Agency. The latter is in pursuit of Giuseppe Gorgiano, a member of an Italian and American criminal society called the Red Circle. They find Gorgiano stabbed to death in the room where the signals came from, and Holmes passes his own signal. Mrs Warren's lodger arrives and announces that she is Emilia Lucca. Her husband, Gennaro, had denounced Gorgiano and his gang in New York, then fled to England, where they had been followed. To ensure their safety they had been living in separate accommodation. Whilst Gennaro was signalling to his wife he had been interrupted by Gorgiano and had killed him before escaping. Leverton is happy with the outcome, and goes to explain this to Scotland Yard.

It seems strange that Gennaro Lucca develops such complicated means of com-

"THEY BUNDLED HIM INTO A CAB THAT WAS BESIDE THE KERB." *Mr Warren is abducted. Illustrated by H.M. Brock and Joseph Simpson.*

munication. He could easily have given a false name at Mrs Warren's and sent letters. If he suspected that the newspaper method was no longer safe and that the house was under surveillance, then it was pointless giving the code and source point for the signals in the same newspaper. This recollection of Holmes's involvement with an American secret society that followed its victims to England must obviously have prompted him to record a longer but very similar occurence only three cases later.

"HOLMES STARED WITH GREAT CURIOSITY AT THE SLIPS OF FOOLSCAP." *And discovers that all isn't what it seems to be (far left).*

"I CAUGHT A GLIMPSE OF A DARK, BEAUTIFUL, HORRIFIED FACE GLARING AT THE NARROW OPENING OF THE BOX-ROOM." *Watson discloses a weakness for Italians.*

THE DISAPPEARANCE OF LADY FRANCES CARFAX

First published: *The Strand Magazine* in December 1911
Main Characters: Lady Frances Carfax, Dr Shlessinger, the Honourable Philip Green, "Holy" Peters

Holmes had been informed that Lady Frances Carfax had, untypically, not been heard of since leaving Lausanne five weeks previously. Watson was sent to Lausanne to investigate and found that Lady Frances had left suddenly after being visited by a tall, dark bearded man. She had apparently travelled to Baden, where she had helped nurse a certain Dr Shlessinger. Watson travelled to Montpellier to question Lady Frances's former maid, who informed him that the bearded stranger had been violent with Lady Frances. Watson was then attacked by the man himself, but was rescued by Holmes in disguise. The stranger was the Honourable Philip Green, who was in love with Lady Frances.

Dr Shlessinger is revealed to be "Holy" Peters, an Australian who preys on the religious feelings of lonely ladies. Peters is

THE STRAND MAGAZINE. Cover for the December 1911 issue containing The Disappearance of Lady Frances Carfax. *The story was illustrated by Alec Ball.*

later found in Brixton where a funeral is being arranged. Holmes forces his way into Peters' house and finds a dead, elderly lady in the coffin before he is ejected by the police. Immediately before the funeral, Holmes and Watson force open the coffin and find Lady Frances drugged on top of the old lady. Holmes had deduced this situation from the great depth of the coffin for such a small lady. Lestrade arrives late with a warrant to find that Peters has escaped in the confusion.

The initial deductions which Holmes makes in this case are amongst the most dubious he ever makes, for there are numerous alternative possibilities available. The case is also an extreme example of the contorted means which some villains will choose to commit murder. The ethical distinctions which Holmes outlines over the drugging are certainly rather weak. The conclusion almost suggests that Holmes was pleased to have a Moriarty substitute still at large to provide future challenges.

THE ADVENTURE OF THE DYING DETECTIVE

First published: *The Strand Magazine* in November 1913
Main Characters: Mrs Hudson, Culverton Smith, Victor Savage, Inspector Morton

Mrs Hudson calls Watson to 221B where she claims that Holmes is dying. Watson finds Holmes gaunt, feverish and occasionally delirious from a disease which he says he has caught from some Chinese sailors. He asks Watson to bring a non-medical expert on the disease, Mr Culverton Smith, to him, but to return alone and ahead of Smith. Smith is reluctant, but agrees when he hears that Holmes is delirious. Watson returns to 221B and Holmes asks him to hide behind the bed. Smith arrives and reveals that he is the cause of Holmes's disease, having sent Holmes a box with a poisoned sharp spring on which Holmes had cut himself. Smith admits that he had done this after finding that Holmes knew too much of the way in which he had killed a Victor Savage. Holmes suddenly revives and Inspector Morton arrives to arrest Smith for the murder of Savage. Smith denies admitting anything to Holmes, but Watson then emerges to conclude the case.

The way in which Holmes convinces Watson that he is delirious is both entertaining and inventive, with his ravings of the world being taken over by oysters. With Holmes's constant concern for those who are ill-treated, he may well have harboured a desire for revenge against the walruses of this world from having read a book which was very popular when he was at college. On a more practical point, it must have been extremely difficult for Watson to have remained hidden behind the bed, and for him to have resisted the urge to rescue Holmes when the latter was being attacked by Smith.

THE VALLEY OF FEAR

First published: *The Strand Magazine* from September 1914 until May 1915
Main Characters: John Douglas, Inspector MacDonald, Professor James Moriarty, Cecil Barker, Mrs Douglas, Hargrave, Ted Baldwin, Bodymaster McGinty, John or "Jack" McMurdo, Ettie Shafter, Birdy Edwards

Holmes receives and decodes a message which implies danger to a John Douglas, whereupon Inspector MacDonald arrives to seek assistance in solving the murder of John Douglas of Birlestone Manor. Holmes suspects that Professor Moriarty is behind the crime, and he travels to Sussex to investigate. Beside the body, the head of which has been blown off with a shotgun, there is a card with "VV 341" on it, and the man's wedding ring has been removed. Douglas had spent many years in America, where he acquired a tattoo on his arm. He had met another Englishman there, Cecil Barker, who was staying with Douglas at the time of the murder.

Barker explains that he heard a single shot, but the only signs of intruders were a footprint on a windowsill and a bicycle abandoned outside the house. Barker suggests that Douglas had been involved with a secret society in America, and mentions that some men had come looking for him soon after he arrived in England. Douglas was always armed, but on the fatal night had left his revolver upstairs. Mrs Douglas states that her husband had lived in dread of a place called the Valley of Fear, and that in a fever he had once called out the name of Bodymaster McGinty. Holmes confounds MacDonald and the local policeman by showing that the slipper worn by Barker exactly fits the footprint on the windowsill.

Watson shortly afterwards sees Mrs Douglas and Barker happily together. Holmes informs Watson that the whole case hangs upon a missing dumb-bell, only one having been found at the scene of the crime, and that he is aware that the stories of Barker and Mrs Douglas are false. The police trace the bicycle to a Mr Hargrave, an American who has disappeared from his nearby hotel. Holmes announces that he is to spend part of the night in the study, and asks MacDonald to inform Barker that he intends having the moat around the house drained. Barker is then seen pulling some clothes from the moat, weighed down by the missing dumb-bell, and marked "Vermissa, USA". These are found to belong to Hargrave's.

Holmes announces that Douglas is not dead, but hiding in the house, and the body is that of his intended assailant, Hargrave. Douglas emerges to describe how he had fought "Hargrave", whose real name was Ted Baldwin, and killed him. Douglas and Barker had used the lodge tattoo on Baldwin's arm, identical to that of Douglas, to pretend that Baldwin was Douglas. Douglas

DUST WRAPPER OF UNIFORM BOOK EDITION. *On this 'Thirties cover Holmes is examining a clue to the murder of John Douglas, not trying on a new shoe.*

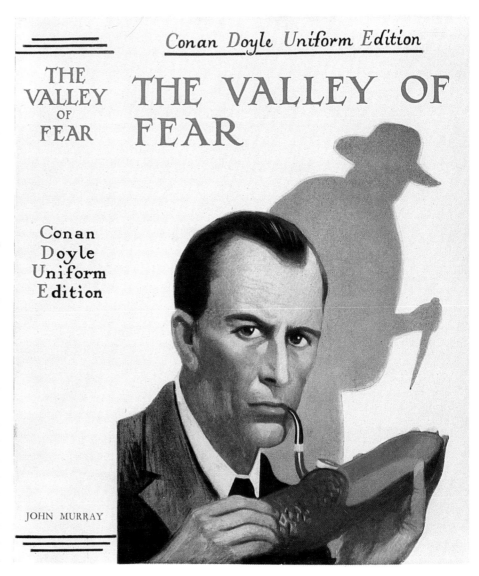

was unable to remove his own wedding ring: hence its absence from the body.

Watson provides an account of events in the Vermissa Valley in America some twenty years earlier, involving a criminally active lodge of a secret sect. The members of this lodge, the "Vermissa Valley – Lodge Number 341" of the "VV 341" card found near Baldwin's body, were known locally as the Scowrers, and they terrorized the inhabitants of the valley. Douglas, a criminal fugitive then known as John or "Jack" McMurdo, joined the lodge, which was run by McGinty. He then fell in love with Ettie Shafter, already promised against her will to Ted Baldwin. McMurdo was soon accepted by the lodge and made privy to all their evil activities. News reached the lodge that Birdy Edwards, a Pinkerton detective, was on their trail and McMurdo was ordered to set a trap for him. When all the leaders of the Scowrers were in one place, McMurdo revealed that he was Birdy Edwards. He had the place surrounded by police and had enough evidence to hang them all. Edwards left the valley with Ettie and her father, but several members of the gang escaped the police and began to hunt for him. He had married Ettie but she later died, and under the name of John Douglas he had moved to England and remarried.

Douglas is acquitted of the murder of Baldwin, but Holmes advises him to leave England, as he believes that Moriarty has been asked to arrange Douglas's death for the remnants of the Scowrers. Two months later Barker informs Holmes that Douglas was lost overboard from a boat travelling to South Africa. Holmes is convinced that it was murder, and that Moriarty's agents were responsible.

In this novel-length case we find Watson once again returning to his predisposition to supply a great deal of information on a wide variety of topics. As with *A Study in Scarlet* and *The Sign of Four*, he provides an excessive amount of detail on what is, after all, only the background to a Holmesian case. In this habit he would, no doubt, have been fully supported by his Literary Agent, who suffered from the same problem. The case itself is a relatively simple one, but it is given far greater depth and significance because of Holmes's perception of the involvement of Moriarty. The information on Moriarty does present difficulties, however, when in the later case of *The Final Problem* Watson says that he knows nothing of Moriarty. It has been claimed by many interested in psychology and, unfortunately, by Holmesian scholars who should know better, that Moriarty may never actually have existed other than in Holmes's mind. It is often claimed, for example, that only Holmes ever sees Moriarty, and in *The Final Problem* this could be accepted. In *The Valley of Fear*, however, Inspector MacDonald actually meets Moriarty, and it is the way in which the professor charms the policeman that should convince us of his cleverness. At the start of this case we also have the statement by Watson that eventually comes close to being realized, when he hopes that he will one day be there to see Holmes and Moriarty have their day.

HIS LAST BOW

First published: *The Strand Magazine* in September 1917
Main Characters: Von Bork, Von Herling, Altamont

In August 1914, Von Bork, the chief German spy in England, meets with Von Herling, the head of the German legation, prior to the former's return to Germany with details of British defences. Von Bork's plans require only information on British naval signalling systems for completion, and these are about to be delivered by Von Bork's best agent, Altamont, a disaffected Irish-American. The latter arrives after the departure of Von Herling for London. Von Bork is tricked into boastingly revealing the combination of his safe before Altamont hands over the naval codes in a package. Von Bork discovers that this package actually contains a copy of Holmes's book, *A Practical Handbook of Bee-Keeping*, just as Altamont chloroforms him. It is then revealed that Altamont is Holmes, and that the chauffeur who delivered him is Watson.

Holmes has spent two years building up his character of Altamont and then feeding Von Bork useless information, whilst arranging the arrest of Von Bork's other agents. Before taking Von Bork to Scotland Yard, Holmes suggests to Watson that this occasion might be their last chance for a quiet talk, and gives a memorable description of the near future and its ultimately better aftermath.

This, chronologically, is the last recorded case of Holmes and Watson. The partnership is well concluded, with Watson rushing to the assistance of his old colleague, in spite of many years of separation, and with Holmes aptly describing Watson as "the one fixed point in a changing age". A question has been raised as to the authorship of this narrative, since it is written in the third person, as opposed to the majority written by Watson. Watson provides us with the answer in *The Problem of Thor Bridge*, where he records that he played so little part in some cases that they must be written "as by a third person".

"HE WAS GRIPPED AT THE BACK OF HIS NECK BY A GRASP OF IRON, AND A CHLOROFORMED SPONGE WAS HELD IN FRONT OF HIS WRITHING FACE." *A disguised Holmes silences the unsuspecting spy before he has a chance to criticize his* Practical Handbook of Bee-Keeping. *Illustrated by Albert Gilbert.*

THE ADVENTURE OF THE MAZARIN STONE

First published: *The Strand Magazine* in October 1921
Main Characters: the Prime Minister, the Home Secretary, Lord Cantlemere, Count Negretto Silvius, Sam Merton

On returning to Baker Street after a long absence, Watson finds that Holmes has been visited by the Prime Minister, the Home Secretary and Lord Cantlemere, who are concerned about the theft of the great yellow Mazarin stone, a Crown diamond. Holmes informs Watson that the stone has been stolen by Count Negretto Silvius, aided by an ex-boxer, Sam Merton.

Holmes sets up a dummy bust of himself in the window, to decoy any murderous attempts on his life. When Silvius calls at 221B, Watson is sent to fetch the police, but Holmes then also calls in Merton from the street. Holmes tells Silvius all the evidence which he has accumulated against him, then leaves them alone in the room while he pretends to play his violin in the next room.

"HIS THICK STICK HALF RAISED, HE WAS CROUCHING FOR HIS FINAL SPRING AND BLOW WHEN A COOL, SARDONIC VOICE GREETED HIM FROM THE OPEN BEDROOM DOOR; 'DON'T BREAK IT!'"
Silvius is fooled by the dummy. The real Holmes stands in the doorway. Illustrated by Albert Gilbert.

He actually plays a record and changes places with the dummy behind the curtain of the window. When Silvius attempts to pass the stone to Merton, Holmes snatches it and the pair are arrested. When Lord Cantlemere calls to check on progress, confidently expecting none, Holmes drops the stone into Lord Cantlemere's pocket and then jokingly suggests that the latter is a receiver of stolen property.

In addition to being one of only two cases recorded in the third person (the other being *His Last Bow*), this is the only case where all of the action takes place in 221B. Holmes is at his most humorous in this case: laughing at a jest made against himself, warning the page boy not to be too rough with the ex-boxer, and tricking Lord Cantlemere. The gramophone which Holmes used must certainly have been an unusual one for that time, too, to have played throughout the whole of the conversation between Silvius and Merton.

THE PROBLEM OF THOR BRIDGE

First published: *The Strand Magazine* in February and March 1922
Main Characters: Neil Gibson, Mrs Gibson, Grace Dunbar, Sergeant Coventry

Holmes is employed by Neil Gibson, a gold-mining magnate, to prove the innocence of Grace Dunbar, the governess of his children, who is accused of murdering his wife. Mrs Gibson's body had been found on a bridge over a mere at their Hampshire estate of Thor Place. She had been shot. A note was found in her hand concerning a meeting with Miss Dunbar on the bridge, and a revolver had been found with one cartridge fired in Miss Dunbar's wardrobe.

Holmes and Watson travel to Thor Place where Holmes notes a chip in the bridge stonework, then they interview Miss Dunbar in Winchester gaol. She reports that Mrs Gibson hated her, suspecting that her husband preferred Miss Dunbar. She had been asked to write the note which was found on the body of Mrs Gibson apparently arranging a rendezvous on Thor Bridge.

On returning to Thor Place, Holmes demonstrates to Watson and Sergeant Coventry, the local policeman, that Mrs Gibson had committed suicide. The revolver had been attached by string to a weight over the mere, chipping the bridge as it flew out of the dead lady's hand. The mate of the revolver had previously been hidden in the wardrobe, and the note kept by Mrs Gibson on her person to incriminate Miss Dunbar.

Holmes produces some of his sharpest remarks in this case, being sarcastic with Watson and deservedly rude to Gibson, again showing his total lack of respect for the powerful and the wealthy. It is rather strange that Holmes is delayed in London to obtain permission to visit a prisoner held in Hampshire, for this permission could have been easily arranged through Miss Dunbar's lawyer in Winchester. Perhaps Holmes was obtaining other information.

THE ADVENTURE OF THE CREEPING MAN

First published: *The Strand Magazine* in March 1923
Main Characters: Trevor Bennett, Professor Presbury, Alice Morphy, Roy the wolfhound

Holmes is informed by Trevor Bennett that Professor Presbury has changed dramatically since his engagement to the much younger Alice Morphy. Without telling his family, the professor had recently travelled to Prague. He had returned with a mysterious small wooden box and was receiving letters marked with an "X" which were only to be opened by him. The professor had been attacked by his faithful wolfhound, Roy, and Bennett had seen the professor crawling on all fours at night. The professor's daughter, Edith, who was also Bennett's fiancée, arrives at 221B to report seeing her father climbing the wall outside her second-floor bedroom window.

Holmes discovers that the professor has been taking a rejuvenation drug developed in Prague, which was derived from a langur, and which had produced simian side effects. On visiting the house at night the professor is found taunting Roy, but the dog's collar slips and the professor is mauled. Holmes criticizes the use of such a potentially dangerous drug and threatens the Hungarian inventor against its continued use.

Holmes appears to have forgotten his own interference with human nature in his earlier days in condemning those, like the professor, who are discontented with their lines. It is interesting to note that an important piece of detective work, in identifying the London intermediary between Presbury and Lowenstein, is commented on by Holmes as merely being routine. It is the work of Holmes's agent, Mercer.

THE ADVENTURE OF THE SUSSEX VAMPIRE

First published: *The Strand Magazine* in January 1924
Main Characters: Robert Ferguson, Mrs Ferguson, Jack Ferguson, Carlo the spaniel

Holmes receives a letter from Robert Ferguson, supposedly about Ferguson's friend, but Holmes deduces that it is about Ferguson himself. Ferguson's Peruvian wife had twice been seen assaulting Jack, his crippled son by a previous marriage. More recently she had twice been seen apparently biting the neck of their own baby, and Ferguson fears vampirism.

Ferguson visits 221B and mentions that Jack is devoted to him but has never shown affection for his step-mother. Visiting the Ferguson home, Holmes finds that their dog, Carlo, has become semi-paralysed, and he carefully examines the South American ornaments of the house. Mrs Ferguson's maid states that her mistress is too ill to see anyone, but when Holmes sends a note upstairs to her she invites him up to see her. Holmes realizes that Mrs Ferguson was sucking poison from a wound and not biting the baby. He had found an empty poisoned-arrow quiver, and deduced that the poison had been tried on the dog. Mrs Ferguson had twice seen the baby being injured with a poisoned arrow, but had refused to say anything because the assailant was the boy, Jack. Holmes suggests that the boy should spend a year at sea.

Perhaps Holmes should have included the recommendation that the voyage should be made on a doomed ship like the *Gloria Scott*, the *Lone Star* or, more appropriately still, the *Palmyra*! It is strange that, rather than risk annoying her husband by reporting Jack's actions, Mrs Ferguson was willing to have her baby remain at risk of being killed. Which did she think would be the worse for her husband to hear?

THE ADVENTURE OF THE THREE GARRIDEBS

First published: *Collier's* in October 1924
Main Characters: John Garrideb, Alexander Garrideb, Nathan Garrideb, Howard Garrideb, "Killer" Evans

COVER FOR *THE STRAND MAGAZINE. The January 1925 issue (right) containing* The Adventure of the Three Garridebs.

"WELL, WE SHALL BE ROUND ABOUT SIX. DR. WATSON WILL COME WITH ME." *Holmes making use of the relatively new invention, the telephone. Illustrated by H.K. Elcock*

John Garrideb informs Holmes that Alexander Garrideb, an American millionaire, had died and left his estate to be divided between any three male Garridebs. None had been found in America, but Nathan Garrideb had been located in London, and it was the latter who wished to bring Holmes into the search. Holmes visits Nathan, who wishes him to find a third Garrideb. John Garrideb then announces that he has found a third, Howard Garrideb, from an advertisement issued in Birmingham. John asks Nathan to go to

Birmingham to obtain an affidavit from Howard.

Holmes and Watson conceal themselves in Nathan's house whilst he is away, and they see John arrive and enter a secret chamber under the floor where counterfeiting equipment is revealed to be hidden. Holmes knocks him out. John, whose real name is "Killer" Evans, had decoyed Nathan away to get at the equipment of a former criminal colleague.

Here we have the use of a telephone at 221B, although there had been earlier references to telephones. It is also in this case that Watson records that Holmes had declined a knighthood. In *The Bruce-Partington Plans* and other cases he does state that he is not interested in honours, but in *The Golden Pince-Nez* it was noted that he had accepted the Legion of Honour. All those who hold this award are Chevaliers of the Order, and thus might technically be considered knights. As a Chevalier, might Holmes, when visiting Miss Adler's (*A Scandel in Bohemia*) district, have been tempted to sing: "Every little scene, seems to whisper Irene"?

THE ADVENTURE OF THE ILLUSTRIOUS CLIENT

First published: *The Strand Magazine* in November 1924
Main Characters: Colonel Sir James Damery, General de Merville, Violet de Merville, Baron Gruner, Shinwell Johnson, Kitty Winter

Colonel Sir James Damery reluctantly informs Holmes that he is acting on behalf of an anonymous benefactor who wishes to help General de Merville in a matter of personal urgency. Holmes is employed to prevent the general's daughter, Violet, from marrying the Austrian murderer, Baron Gruner. Holmes informs Gruner that he does intend to prevent the wedding, and is threatened in return. One of Holmes's agents, a reformed ex-convict called Shinwell Johnson, introduces Holmes to Kitty Winter, who seeks revenge against Gruner for being abandoned by him after an affair. She informs Holmes that Gruner keeps a book listing his female conquests.

Holmes and Kitty attempt to persuade Violet against Gruner, but she is so infatuated that she will not believe accounts of his previous ill-treatment of women. Holmes is then attacked, but feigns worse injuries. Watson is sent to Gruner's house to divert him with an offer of a Ming saucer for his collection. Holmes takes Kitty to help him find Gruner's book, but she throws acid in Gruner's face, blinding and disfiguring him. Kitty receives a minimal sentence and Violet ends the affair.

In this case Holmes reveals some important clues about his attitudes towards women. It is strange that he does not force the full disclosure of the identity of the "illustrious client" who actually has made Damery present the case to Holmes. There are indications that this might have been Edward VII himself. This case has some peculiar inclusions. Why, for example, does Holmes have his jacket with him in the Turkish Bath?

THE ADVENTURE OF THE THREE GABLES

First published: *Liberty* in September 1926
Main Characters: Steve Dixie, Barney Stockdale, Mary Maberley, Susan, Douglas Maberley, Langdale Pike, Isadora Klein, the Duke of Lomond

Holmes is dramatically threatened not to intrude in affairs at Harrow by Steve Dixie, a negro boxer, supposedly on the orders of Barney Stockdale. Holmes intimidates Dixie with his knowledge of the latter's criminal activities. Mrs Maberley of Harrow had already asked Holmes to investigate the suspiciously high price she had been offered for her house, provided that she leaves most of the contents of the house within it. When Holmes discovers that Mrs Maberley's maid, Susan, has been spying on her, the latter leaves the household immediately. Mrs Maberley's son, Douglas, had died of pneumonia in Rome the previous month, and some of his papers are taken when the house is burgled, although one page, revealing that it had been part of a dramatic novel, had accidentally dropped out on to the floor.

Holmes discoveres from Langdale Pike, a well-known social gossip-monger, that Douglas had been the lover of Isadora Klein, an extremely wealthy and beautiful widow who is about to marry the young Duke of Lomond. Isadora reluctantly admits to Holmes that after she had eventually rejected Douglas, he had written a novel about their affair and had sent her one of the two copies to let her know of the

contents. She had been attempting to obtain the other copy by buying the house containing it. Holmes allows her to keep the other copy in exchange for a trip around the world for Mrs Maberley.

This case has generated a great deal of comment about Holmes's seemingly racial attitude to Steve Dixie. Although all claims of prejudice can be explained away, it is difficult to excuse the natural interpretation. Although he suggests that Dixie is compounding a felony, as he himself does in several other cases, Dixie is not actually guilty of that crime, but of "misprision of felony", the concealing of a felony.

THE ADVENTURE OF THE BLANCHED SOLDIER

First published: *Liberty* in October 1926
Main Characters: James Dodd, Godfrey Emsworth, Colonel Emsworth, Mrs Emsworth, Sir James Saunders

James Dodd informs Holmes that his Army friend, Godfrey Emsworth, had been wounded in South Africa, and that only vague information could be obtained about the present location of Godfrey from his father, Colonel Emsworth. After visiting Godfrey's mother, Dodd had caught a glimpse of Godfrey, who was looking very blanched in colour and appeared to be restrained in a small house in the grounds of the Emsworth estate.

Holmes visits Colonel Emsworth with Dodd and an anonymous accomplice, and informs him that he knows why Godfrey is being hidden. He passes the Colonel a note with the single word "leprosy" on it, and Godfrey is brought to the house. After being wounded he had unknowingly slept in a leper hospital, and then developed the symptoms when he returned to England. Holmes's companion, Sir James Saunders, is an expert on the disease, and he diagnoses that Godfrey has the non-contagious disease of pseudo-leprosy.

"HE SPRANG BACK WHEN HE SAW THAT I WAS LOOKING AT HIM AND VANISHED INTO THE DARKNESS." *In this story, recorded by Holmes, James Dodd explains how he was startled by the pale figure of his lost friend Godfrey.*

This is one of the two cases which Holmes records himself, and Watson plays no active part in it. It will be seen that it is very much

in the same style as that of Watson, in spite of Holmes's frequent criticisms of that style elsewhere. Holmes also has to admit that Watson's absence presents him with difficulties in narrating the case. It appears too that Holmes suffers from the same problem as Watson in connection with his remembrance of railway journeys, for he claims that he set off for Bedford from Euston, when the London terminus for that town is St Pancras. The case has a key reference to the possibility of a second wife for Watson.

THE ADVENTURE OF THE LION'S MANE

First published: *Liberty* in November 1926
Main Characters: Harold Stackhurst, Fitzroy McPherson, Ian Murdoch, Maud Bellamy, Inspector Bardle

This narrative is recorded by Holmes himself, and Watson plays no active part in it. Holmes relates how, whilst walking from his retirement home on the South Downs to the beach, he had met Harold Stackhurst, a local headmaster. They discovered Fitzroy McPherson, another teacher from Stackhurst's establishment, who was wearing a swimming costume and was covered in whip-like marks. McPherson muttered "the lion's mane" and then died. Ian Murdoch, another teacher, arrived and behaved in a rather suspicious manner. Holmes and Stackhurst visited Maud Bellamy, McPherson's fiancée, but she was unable to help.

Stackhurst dismissed Murdoch from his school because he would not divulge information which he appeared to have in connection with the mystery. A week later, McPherson's dog is found dead near where his master died. Inspector Bardle suggested that Murdoch should be arrested, but as Holmes was explaining that there was in fact no case against him, the very man arrived, covered in marks like those of McPherson. Holmes showed Bardle and Stackhurst that the "murderer" was a poisonous jellyfish which looks like a lion's mane. Murdoch had survived the attack because he was fitter, and he explained that he had appeared to behave suspiciously because he did not wish to reveal that he had loved Maud Bellamy.

Holmes appears to contradict one of his earliest statements about himself here. In *A Study in Scarlet* he had stated that only a fool stored every piece of information in the attic of his brain, whereas here he states that his brain is like a crowded box-room. What he does not explain is how he differentiates between the trifles which might be useful later, and those which might not. At the conclusion of the case he quite rightly criticizes himself, but for the wrong reason. He states that the unused towel misled him into believing that McPherson had not been in the water. Immediately after McPherson's death, however, he correctly deduced that McPherson had either not been in the water or had not bothered drying himself. It was this second option which Holmes forgot.

THE ADVENTURE OF THE RETIRED COLOURMAN

First published: *Liberty* in December 1926
Main Characters: Josiah Amberley, Mrs Amberley, Dr Ray Ernest, Inspector McKinnon

Josiah Amberley, a retired manufacturer of painting materials, informs Holmes that he had married a woman twenty years younger than himself, and that she had become intimate with his chess-playing acquaintance, Dr Ray Ernest. Mrs Amberley had

THE STRAND MAGAZINE, January 1927, the New Year edition featuring the first British publication of The Adventure of the Retired Colourman.

recently disappeared with Amberley's money. Watson is sent to investigate the affair, but notes nothing unusual except a strong smell of paint in the house. Amberley visits Holmes again, having received a telegram summoning him to a small village in Essex. Watson and Amberley travel to the village and find that the telegram was a hoax. When they return the next day, Holmes accuses Amberley of murdering his wife and her suspected lover. Amberley fails to kill himself and is arrested.

Holmes visits Amberley's house with Inspector McKinnon the next day and explains that he had diverted Amberley to Essex in order to search Amberley's house. He had found a gas-pipe leading into a gas-tight room, where he had found the start of a note written low down on a wall, and had deduced that Amberley had gassed the lovers and then disposed of the bodies. The fresh paint had been used to hide the residual smell of the gas. The bodies are later found in a disused well.

This case contains an example of a problem which must have occurred several times in the course of Holmes's career. He hands over the glory for solving the case to Inspector McKinnon, but then mentions that Watson might be able to write up the case later. Such an account, as this particular one demonstrates, would inevitably reveal that the police did not deserve the credit for solving the case. There is a problem when Holmes suggests that a pencil might later be found on one of the bodies. Anyone who had become unconscious in the middle of writing a sentence would either have the pencil in their hand, where Amberley would almost certainly have seen it, or else it would have dropped onto the floor, where Amberley or Holmes would have found it. The writer would certainly not have replaced it in his pocket.

THE ADVENTURE OF THE VEILED LODGER

First published: *Liberty* in January 1927
Main Characters: Mrs Merrilow, Eugenia Ronder, Mr Ronder, Leonardo

Mrs Merrilow, a landlady from South Brixton, informs Holmes that her solitary lodger, Eugenia Ronder, has a disfigured face which she keeps veiled. Her lodger has avoided society and has lately been disturbed by dreams involving murder and been heard shouting "coward" in her sleep.

Holmes recalls that the Ronders had been show-people and that an accident had occured seven years before wherein Mr Ronder had been killed by an escaped lion and Mrs Ronder badly mauled.

When Holmes and Watson visit Mrs Ronder she informs them that her husband had ill-treated her and that her lover, Leonardo, had killed Ronder with a club fitted with nails to simulate a lion's claw. When, as planned, Mrs Ronder freed the lion, it unexpectedly attacked her, and Leonardo fled in fear. As Leonardo had recently died, Eugenia wished to have the truth recorded before she might die. Holmes gently warns her against thoughts of suicide and she accepts his advice.

This is the shortest of the Holmes narratives, occupying less than six pages of text when later published in *The Strand Magazine,* but it includes an important point. The seventeen years of collaboration mentioned by Watson must be fitted between 1881, when they met, and 1903. In addition to the missing three years after Reichenbach there are two years unaccounted for, which can be explained by means of a misreading of a doctor's "19" as a "17", or by Watson being absent on Army medical duties during some of the Canonically non-busy years of the Boer Wars. Holmes's more sympathetic side is well demonstrated in the advice which he gives to Eugenia, and in the pride which he takes in her response.

THE ADVENTURE OF SHOSCOMBE OLD PLACE

First published: *Liberty* in March 1927
Main Characters: Sir Robert Norberton, Lady Beatrice Falder, John Mason,
"Shoscombe Prince"

Holmes asks for information on Sir Robert Norberton, and Watson recalls that Sir Robert had once horse-whipped a money-lender, and that his home at Shoscombe Old Place is his racehorse training centre. The house is owned by his widowed sister, Lady Beatrice Falder, who also lives there and who breeds spaniels.

Norberton's head trainer, John Mason, visits 221B and reports that he considers Sir Robert to have gone mad, partly from the strain of knowing that his fate depends entirely on his horse, Shoscombe Prince, winning the Derby. Norberton had recently given Lady Beatrice's favourite spaniel away for no apparent reason, and had been meeting a mysterious man in the crypt of the old church. Lady Beatrice, too, appears to have changed her character. Mason had now found some ancient human remains in the crypt.

Holmes and Watson travel to Shoscombe, supposedly on a fishing trip. The next day they borrow Lady Beatrice's favourite spaniel from its new owner, the local publican, for a walk. The dog runs to Lady Beatrice's carriage but snaps at the lady inside. When Holmes visits the crypt he finds, as he expected, that the remains have gone, and as he opens one of the tombs he is interrupted by Sir Robert's arrival. Norberton admits that the tomb contains Lady Beatrice's body, as she had died a week previously of natural causes. If the death had been announced at the time, Norberton would have lost his horse to the money-lender he had once attacked. The husband of Lady Beatrice's maid had been impersonating Lady Beatrice until the race, when she would have been given a proper burial. Shoscombe Prince does win the Derby and Sir Robert re-establishes himself.

It is strange that the last case which was recorded about Holmes's exploits should be one of those in which no serious crime is actually committed. There is a nice touch of character in connection with Watson's admission that he loses half of his wound pension on horseracing. A less endearing trait is revealed when Watson finds it difficult to accept that a member of the minor nobility might have murdered his own sister, considering all the previous experiences with the nobility which Watson had recorded. It appears that Watson still would not learn from experience, but then, as Holmes states in the chronologically last case of their adventures together, *His Last Bow,* Watson never changes.

SIR ARTHUR CONAN DOYLE

A Brief Biographical Study
Christopher Roden

SIR ARTHUR CONAN DOYLE

Although the world has chosen to remember Sir Arthur Conan Doyle chiefly for his creation of the fictional master detective, Sherlock Holmes, his life, like the literary canvas which he painted, was varied and highly interesting.

Arthur Conan Doyle was born in Edinburgh on 22nd May 1859. His mother, Mary, was of Irish extraction and traced her ancestry back to the famous Percy family of Northumberland and from there to the Plantagenet line. It is little wonder that the young Conan Doyle was told tales steeped in history which were to stand him in good stead when, in later years, he was to write his famous historical novels *The White Company*, *Sir Nigel* and *Micah Clarke*.

The family was a large one – Arthur was one of ten Doyle children, seven of whom survived to maturity – and life was difficult for his mother who struggled to bring up the children on the income of some £240 a year provided by her husband, Charles, who pursued an unambitious life as a civil servant. Charles Altamont Doyle was the youngest son of John Doyle, the caricaturist "H.B." His brothers had all made something of a name for themselves: James Doyle wrote *The Chronicles of England*; Henry Doyle became the manager of the National Gallery in Dublin; and Richard Doyle became famous for his cover design for *Punch*. Whilst Charles Doyle also had artistic talents, he exercised his skills only intermittently, and lack of drive led to the loss of his post as a civil servant in the Office of Works at Edinburgh. After this he lapsed steadily into alcoholism, and his epilepsy grew increasingly worse, so that he was institutionalized for the final ten years of his life, and died in 1893.

The effect on Conan Doyle of his father's alcoholism and institutionalisation was profound and, whilst he chose to draw a veil over this particular topic in his autobiography *Memories and Adventures*, alcoholism is dealt with rather severely when it appears in his later fictional writings.

Conan Doyle's education took place at home and in a local Edinburgh school until, at the age of nine, he was sent to the Jesuit

MARY DOYLE, *Conan Doyle's mother, in 1891 at the age of 53.*

CONAN DOYLE *demonstrating a ROC motorbike at Undershaw, his home in Surrey, February 1905 (opposite).*

THE *STRAND* ON DOYLE. *The article, December 1891, appeared five months after the* Strand *started publishing the Holmes stories.*

preparatory school of Hodder in Lancashire. Hodder was attached to the Jesuit secondary school of Stonyhurst, and it was to this school that Conan Doyle moved after two years. The time spent at Stonyhurst was not a particularly happy one, although the records show that the young Doyle was a better than average performer. The spartan surroundings and the Jesuit discipline did not appeal to Doyle, and it appears that he experienced his fair share of corporal punishment.

It was at Stonyhurst that Conan Doyle began seriously to examine his religious beliefs and, by the time he left the school in 1875, he had firmly rejected Christianity and had become an agnostic. The turmoil and questioning which must have taken place in his own mind is dealt with in some detail in his semi-autobiographical novel *The Stark Munro Letters*.

After leaving Stonyhurst, Conan Doyle spent a further year with the Jesuits in Feldkirch, Austria, before returning to Edinburgh to study medicine at the University from 1876 to 1881. Besides providing him with a medical degree, Edinburgh University also brought Conan Doyle into contact with two characters who were to be important models for future fictional creations: Professor Rutherford, whose Assyrian beard, prodigious voice, enormous chest and singular manner became translated into the character of Professor George Edward Challenger of *The Lost World*; and Dr Joseph Bell, whose amazing deductions of the history of his various patients were to

THE STONYHURST CRICKET CLUB 1873. Conan Doyle, an accomplished cricketer, is standing far right.

upkeep of the family, jobs which, as a medical assistant, took him to Sheffield, Birmingham and Shropshire, and further afield to the Arctic where he served as ship's doctor aboard a Greenland whaler. Immediately following his term at university, he was to serve as a ship's doctor on a voyage to the West African coast.

In 1882, the enigmatic Dr George Turnavine Budd, who Doyle had first met when the two were students in Edinburgh, invited him to become his partner in a medical practice in Plymouth. Their relationship was a turbulent one, and ended with Doyle moving to Southsea. It is perhaps fortunate for us that the break occurred when it did, for, although he built up a relatively successful medical practice, it was during his quieter moments at Southsea that Doyle expanded his literary activities – leading eventually to the creation of Sherlock Holmes and the detective's first appearance in *A Study in Scarlet*, which appeared in *Beeton's Christmas Annual* for 1887.

Following the acceptance of *A Study in Scarlet*, for which he was paid the paltry sum of £25, Conan Doyle decided to test his powers to the full with a long historical novel. The outcome was the highly successful *Micah Clarke*, which finally appeared in 1889. It must have been pleasing to Conan

provide the ideas behind the deductive skills of Sherlock Holmes.

Whilst at Edinburgh, Conan Doyle took various jobs to assist his mother with the

BEETON'S CHRISTMAS ANNUAL, 1887, containing A Study in Scarlet, *the first of the Sherlock Holmes stories.*

DR JOSEPH BELL *(above), Conan Doyle's tutor at Edinburgh University, whose exceptional powers of observation were, in part, the inspiration for Sherlock Holmes.*

LOUISA HAWKINS *("Touie") (above right), Conan Doyle's first wife, who died on 4th July 1906, was a sister of one of his patients. Touie was very supportive of Doyle's earlier literary efforts.*

Doyle that the novel became a topic of conversation between himself and Oscar Wilde when the two met, along with J.M. Stoddart of *Lippincott's Monthly Magazine* for a dinner in the summer of 1889; a dinner which ended with Conan Doyle receiving a commission to write a further Sherlock Holmes adventure (*The Sign of the Four*), and Wilde the commission for *The Picture of Dorian Gray*.

Meanwhile, other events had occurred in Conan Doyle's life which were to influence his actions and beliefs for many years to come. In 1885, he married Louise Hawkins ("Touie") whose constant poor health was to lead to frequent domestic upheaval in the forthcoming years, and in 1886 he began to develop an interest in psychic studies following meetings which he had attended in Southsea.

By 1890, Conan Doyle had resolved that a change was necessary and that he would journey to Vienna to study the eye. By the spring of 1891, the Doyles were back in London, renting rooms in Montague Place whilst Conan Doyle looked around for a suitable office to put up his plate as an oculist. He eventually found accommodation at 2 Devonshire Place. The patients did not come, however, and, without even a ring at the doorbell to disturb him, he was able to devote his time to writing.

It was fortuitous that *The Strand Magazine* first saw publication about this time, in January 1891, and that Conan Doyle took the opportunity on hand to revive the Sherlock Holmes of his two successful novels for a series of adventures. *A Scandal in Bohemia* was the first to appear, in July 1891. Doyle continued to contribute adventures featuring Sherlock Holmes to *The Strand Magazine* but nonetheless, while he was writing these Holmes stories, he was anxious that he should be writing books that would make his a "lasting name in English literature". In November 1891, he wrote to his mother: "I think of slaying Holmes . . . and winding him up for good and all. He takes my mind from better things."

The idea of Holmes's death remained with him, and it seems that it was during a visit to Switzerland in 1893 that Doyle was shown the Reichenbach Falls, which he was subsequently to choose as the location for the "fatal" struggle with Moriarty. *The Final Problem*, the adventure which was to bring the news of Sherlock Holmes's death to a horrified nation, appeared in *The Strand Magazine* in December 1893. It is with the apparent death of the great detective that we can best leave the relationship between Conan Doyle and Holmes in order to concentrate on the many other varied events which filled Conan Doyle's life.

The tuberculosis to which Touie had become prey had completely disorganized the lives of the couple, and it was hoped that a winter in Egypt might effect a cure. The Doyles left England in the autumn of 1895 and journeyed to Cairo. The surroundings were to provide Conan Doyle with his plot

THE STRAND MAGAZINE, *July 1891, containing* A Scandal in Bohemia, *the first Sherlock Holmes short story and the first to be illustrated by Sidney Paget (left).*

for the desert drama *The Tragedy of the Korosko*, which first appeared in 1898. It was during this visit to Egypt that fighting broke out between the British and the Dervishes, and Conan Doyle seized the opportunity which presented itself to cable *The Westminster Gazette* asking to be appointed their honorary war correspondent. In this capacity he made his way to the front to witness the action at first hand: an experience which would equip him well for similar involvement in war, and war reporting, in later years.

Shortly after their return to England, the Doyles moved into a new house which Sir Arthur had had built at Hindhead in Surrey – an area chosen because it was believed that the air of the Surrey countryside would be beneficial to the health of the ailing Touie. Meanwhile, Conan Doyle's literary output continued unabated and, during this period, he produced his famous novel of the Regency, *Rodney Stone*; a tale of early married life, *A Duet with an Occasional Chorus*; and his Napoleonic portrait, *Uncle Bernac*.

In late December 1899, Conan Doyle once more became involved with warfare as the shadow of the problems in South Africa

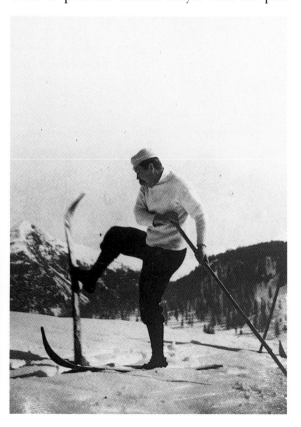

CONAN DOYLE *demonstrating his Norwegian skis at Davos Platz in 1894, The first time that such skis were introduced to Switzerland (left below).*

THE LANGHAM HOSPITAL STAFF *in 1900, preparing to leave for the Boer War. Conan Doyle is third from the left.*

A STUDY IN SCARLET PAPERBACK *presented with the* Windsor Magazine *Christmas edition, 1895, illustrated by James Greig.*

was cast over Britain. Anxious to serve his country, he attempted to enlist with the Middlesex Yeomanry and was devastated when their only response was to place him on a waiting list. Almost immediately, however, he was contacted by John Langman who was sending out a hospital of 50 beds, at his own expense, to Africa. Langman suggested that Conan Doyle should help him to choose the personnel and that he should also supervise the entire operation in an unofficial capacity. Keen to serve in whatever way he could, Conan Doyle accepted enthusiastically.

The Langman hospital sailed for Cape Town in February 1900, reaching its destination on 21st March. Conan Doyle was to spend his next months in the filth of the enteric hospital. He wrote:

Our hospital was no worse off than the others, and as there were many of them the general condition of the town was very bad. Coffins were out of the question, and the men were lowered in their brown blankets into shallow graves at the average rate of sixty a day. A sickening smell came from the stricken town. Once when I had ridden out to get an hour or two of change, and was at least six miles from the town, the wind changed and the smell was all around me. You could smell Bloemfontein long before you could see it. Even now if I felt that lowly death smell compounded of disease and disinfectants my heart would sink within me.

Before returning to England in the August of 1901, Conan Doyle joined the forces in South Africa, an experience which was to contribute to his knowledge of the war and enable him to write and publish *The History of the Great Boer War*.

Following the war, an extraordinary outbreak of defamation had occurred around the world over Britain's conduct, and this prompted Conan Doyle to write a short pamphlet, *The War in South Africa: Its Causes and Conduct*, which was widely translated. Doyle held the opinion that it was the reaction engendered by this pamphlet that resulted in his being knighted, and appointed as Deputy-Lieutenant of Surrey, in 1902.

During the early years of the twentieth century, Conan Doyle twice stood for Parliament, once in Edinburgh and once in the Border Burghs. On both occasions he turned in a respectable vote, although he was not returned. In later years, he was to comment on the rigours of campaigning for office:

It is a vile business this electioneering, though no doubt it is chastening in its effects. They say that mud-baths are healthy and purifying, and I can compare it to nothing else. This applies, particularly, I think, to Scotland, where the art of heckling has been carried to extremes ... The electors have returned me to the bosom of my family. A very pleasant constituency it is. I had now thoroughly explored that path, and had assured myself that my life's journey did not lie along it. And yet I was deeply convinced that public service was waiting for me somewhere. One likes to feel that one has some small practical influence upon the affairs of one's time, but I encourage myself by the thought that though I have not been a public man, my utterances in several pamphlets and numerous letters in the Press may have had more weight with the public since I was disassociated from any political interest which could sway my judgment.

Following the death of Touie in 1906 Conan Doyle entered a period of blackness, during which he was unable to settle to work until a case, in which he considered there had been a grave miscarriage of justice, came to his attention.

George Edalji's story began in 1903. Edalji's father, a Parsee turned Christian, had been vicar of the parish of Great Wyrley, a mining district near Birmingham, for almost 30 years. The father had married an Englishwoman and the family had become the butt of practical jokes and menacing anonymous letters. Even though these letters threatened the family, it was con-

sidered by the Chief Constable of Staffordshire that they were written by George. When the key of the local grammar school was found on the Edaljis' doorstep, the Chief Constable wrote to Edalji's father that he knew George had been responsible, and that "he hoped to give the culprit a dose of penal servitude". Although this latter incident occurred in 1895 it had obviously been kept in mind for, when an outbreak of savage attacks on horses and cattle occurred in the district in 1903, a new spate of anonymous letters began; letters which accused George of being one of a gang of cattle killers. The family home was searched, some dubious evidence uncovered, and this resulted in George Edalji being sentenced to seven years' imprisonment.

Conan Doyle first came across the case in late 1906 and, so convinced was he at the apparent injustice to Edalji, that he began a series of articles on "The Case of George Edalji" which appeared in the *Daily Telegraph* from January 1907 onwards. Of Edalji, Doyle wrote:

If the whole land had been raked, I do not think that it would have been possible to find a man who was so unlikely, and indeed so incapable, of committing such actions. He was of irreproachable character. Nothing in his life had ever been urged against him. His old schoolmaster with years of experience testified to his mild and tractable disposition. He had served his time with a Birmingham solicitor, who gave him the highest references. He had never shown traits of cruelty. He was so devoted to his work that he had won the highest honours in the legal classes, and he had already at the age of twenty-seven written a book upon Railway Law. Finally he was a total abstainer, and so blind that he was unable to recognize any one at the distance of six yards. It was clear that the inherent improbability of such a man committing a long succession of bloody and brutal crimes was so great that it could only be met by the suggestion of insanity. There had never, however, been any indication even of eccentricity in George Edalji. On the contrary, his statements of defence were measured and rational, and he had come through a series of experiences which might well have unhinged a weaker intellect.

Conan Doyle's investigations and articles caused a storm of indignation throughout the country. A Government committee was formed to report on the case but, although they were severe on the condemnation of Edalji, they held to the theory that he had written the anonymous letters and, therefore, denied him any compensation for his

GEORGE EDALJI (*left*) *and his case of injustice became one of Conan Doyle's famous causes.*

131

long period of suffering. Others felt differently and the Law Society, who had barred Edalji from practising, immediately re-admitted him to their roll of solicitors, and the *Daily Telegraph* began a subscription for him which raised some £300.

Conan Doyle married Miss Jean Leckie in 1907. The two had met as early as 1897 and had maintained a respectable friendship throughout the years of Touie's illness. They had fallen in love as soon as they met, and it is much to the credit of both of them, and an indication of Conan Doyle's own moral attitude, that their relationship remained purely platonic until their marriage. George Edalji was one of the guests at the wedding reception. Doyle wrote, "there was no guest whom I was prouder to see".

Shortly following their marriage, the Conan Doyles moved to Crowborough in Sussex and it was at Windlesham that they were to live for their remaining years. However, Conan Doyle's name was to be in the forefront of the public's mind for some time to come. In 1910, he became involved in a second case of injustice – this time that

of Oscar Slater, a German Jew, wrongfully accused of murder. The case was long and protracted, with Slater serving an eighteen-year term of imprisonment until finally, in 1927, he was released and awarded £6,000 compensation. Doyle described Slater as "not a very desirable member of Society" but, nevertheless, he pursued the case as vigorously as that of Edalji. At the very end, there was disagreement between Conan Doyle and Slater over the money which Conan Doyle had expended in Slater's cause – a disagreement which was never settled.

In 1912, Conan Doyle was to introduce another famous character into the world of literature with the appearance of Professor

JEAN LECKIE (right) at the time when she first met Conan Doyle. An old friend, she was to become the second Lady Conan Doyle in 1907.

ARTHUR AND JEAN DOYLE IN EGYPT (below) during a Mediterranean cruise. The Doyles greatly enjoyed travel and experiencing different cultures. In later years Conan Doyle spent much time abroad lecturing on Spiritualism.

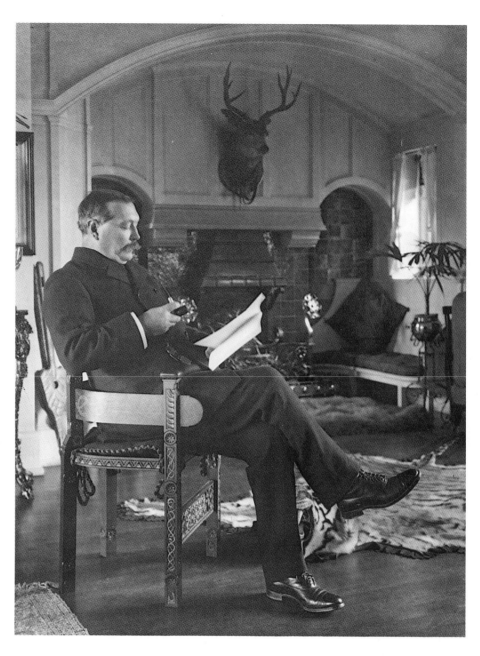

Challenger in *The Lost World*, a tale of pre-history, alive and surviving on a remote South American plateau. Challenger was to have further adventures, including *The Poison Belt* which appeared in the following year.

The impending war with Germany was much in Doyle's mind at this time, and it was during this period that he began to advocate the need for a Channel tunnel – a dream that has taken some three-quarters of a century to realize.

With the outbreak of the First World War in 1914, Conan Doyle was instrumental in forming the local volunteer force which was shortly to be re-formed as an official body. Doyle served as a private in the Crowborough Company of the Sixth Royal Sussex Volunteer Regiment. In 1915, he began writing his six-volume history of *The British Campaign in France and Flanders*, which was completed in 1920. Once more, in the role of a war journalist, Conan Doyle visited the battle fronts of the British, French and Italians, where he was to meet and talk with Haig and other generals.

By 1916, Conan Doyle's explorations into psychic matters had convinced him that he should devote the final years of his life to the advancement of Spiritualism. He began to write extensively on the subject, and to travel the world with his family promoting his beliefs. From those who had lost loved ones during the First World War he found a ready acceptance for his arguments, but his beliefs were to bring him into conflict with many people during the course of the final thirteen years of his life.

Spiritualism became Conan Doyle's religion and his driving force, taking him to Australia, America, Canada and South Africa for lecture tours which he recorded in various autobiographical studies. He was careful in his testing of mediums but, not unnaturally, those cases where he was deceived have been seized upon by critics to justify what they regard as his credulity. Credulity was a charge also to be levelled at

CONAN DOYLE *(above) sitting in the music room at Windlesham, 1912. Photographed by E.O. Hoppe.*

PROFESSOR CHALLENGER *(above left). Cover for the* Sunday Magazine *of the* New York Tribune *containing the first part of the American serialization of* The Lost World, *March 1912. The model for the cover was Conan Doyle.*

CONAN DOYLE AND SONS *Denis and Malcolm (Adrian). Doyle had his uniform custom-made for his part in the First World War (right).*

DOYLE IN SEARCH OF FAIRIES *(above). With a gramophone to lure the fairies out of hiding, Doyle takes along Elsie Ezra, the gardener's daughter, believing that the sprites were more visible to the eyes of children.*

THE DOYLE FAMILY AND HOUDINI *(in the centre) on the beach at Atlantic City in 1922. Lady Jean, a sometime clairvoyant, claimed to have seen the escapologist's dead mother in a vision bearing a crucifix. After hearing this, Houdini, who was Jewish, called an end to his brief friendship with the Doyles.*

FRANCES GRIFFITHS AND THE FAIRIES. *The controversial photograph taken by Elsie Wright, July 1917.*

Doyle when, in 1922, he declared the famous Cottingley Fairy photographs to be genuine. This latter case has been frequently documented, and the photographs are famous the world over. Briefly, it concerns claims made in 1917 by Elsie Wright and her cousin Frances Griffiths that they had returned home, late for tea, because they had been playing with fairies. To back up their claims, they borrowed a box camera and produced photographs of themselves with the fairies. Edward Gardner, a leading Theosophist who saw the photographs, was convinced of their authenticity and brought the case to Conan Doyle's attention. It has to be said in defence of Doyle, however, that the investigations into the photographs were carried out by third parties and we should not lose sight of what he wrote:

If I am asked whether I consider the case to be absolutely and finally proved, I should answer that in order to remove the faint shadow of doubt I should wish to see the result repeated before a disinterested witness.

SPIRIT "EXTRA" OF CONAN DOYLE. *Lady Conan Doyle and Denis are joined by an apparition of the deceased writer. The photographer was William Hope, 1931.*

135

THE DOYLES AT WITTERING, 1922. *From left to right: Malcolm (Adrian), Billie (Lena Jean), Sir Arthur, Denis, and Doyle's private secretary, Major A.H. Wood.*

SIR ARTHUR AND LADY JEAN *in Grindelwald, 1924.*

Following a tour of Scandinavia and Holland in 1929, Conan Doyle returned to England exhausted and suffered a heart attack. He remained weak and ill for several months and died at home on 7th July 1930.

Conan Doyle's contribution to the literature of the English language was immense. His major historical novels *The White Company, Sir Nigel, Micah Clarke, Uncle Bernac, The Refugees* and *The Great Shadow* are perhaps less well known today than the remarkable number of short stories, written chiefly for the popular magazines of his time: *Tales of Adventure and Medical Life, Tales of the Ring and Camp, Tales of Pirates and Blue Water* and tales of horror and the supernatural. His major fictional creations, Sherlock Holmes, Professor Challenger and Brigadier Gerard, have collections of stories all of their own, collections which will continue to be read and enjoyed the world over for very many years to come.

Above all, perhaps, Conan Doyle should be remembered for his energy and variety of talents. He was a fine sportsman – at cricket he once captured the wicket of the great W.G. Grace, a feat which inspired him to write a poem on the subject; he played football, rugby and golf, and was sufficiently innovative to introduce cross-country skiing to Switzerland. He wrote to the newspapers on all manner of topics, was always a strong campaigner for the underdog, and had a keen interest in photography which enabled him to contribute authoritative articles to *The British Journal of Photography*.

Whenever we read the adventures of Sherlock Holmes and Doctor Watson, we encounter Sir Arthur Conan Doyle – for there is something of the great man in all his writings.

CONAN DOYLE BOOKMARK (*above*), *from a cigarette card, circa 1910.*

CONAN DOYLE AND EILLE NORWOOD *at the Stoll Films Convention dinner at the Trocadero Ballroom, 1921.*

THE CANON TODAY

A STUDY IN SCARLET
Published as a novel in 1888

THE SIGN OF FOUR
Published as a novel in 1890

THE ADVENTURES OF SHERLOCK HOLMES
Published as a collection in 1892
A Scandal in Bohemia
The Red-Headed League
A Case of Identity
The Boscombe Valley Mystery
The Five Orange Pips
The Man with the Twisted Lip
The Adventure of the Blue Carbuncle
The Adventure of the Speckled Band
The Adventure of the Engineer's Thumb
The Adventure of the Noble Bachelor
The Adventure of the Beryl Coronet
The Adventure of the Copper Beeches

THE MEMOIRS OF SHERLOCK HOLMES
Published as a collection in 1894
Silver Blaze
The Yellow Face
The Stock-Broker's Clerk
The "Gloria Scott"
The Musgrave Ritual
The Reigate Squires
The Crooked Man
The Resident Patient
The Greek Interpreter
The Naval Treaty
The Final Problem

THE HOUND OF THE BASKERVILLES
Published as a novel in 1902

THE RETURN OF SHERLOCK HOLMES
Published as a collection in 1905
The Adventure of the Empty House
The Adventure of the Norwood Builder
The Adventure of the Dancing Men
The Adventure of the Solitary Cyclist
The Adventure of the Priory School
The Adventure of Black Peter
The Adventure of Charles Augustus Milverton
The Adventure of the Six Napoleons
The Adventure of the Three Students
The Adventure of the Golden Pince-Nez
The Adventure of the Missing Three-Quarter
The Adventure of the Abbey Grange
The Adventure of the Second Stain

THE VALLEY OF FEAR
Published as a novel in 1915

HIS LAST BOW
Published as a collection in 1917
The Adventure of Wisteria Lodge
The Adventure of the Cardboard Box
The Adventure of the Red Circle
The Adventure of the Bruce-Partington Plans
The Adventure of the Dying Detective
The Disappearance of Lady Frances Carfax
The Adventure of the Devil's Foot
His Last Bow

THE CASE-BOOK OF SHERLOCK HOLMES
Published as a collection in 1927
The Adventure of the Illustrious Client
The Adventure of the Blanched Soldier
The Adventure of the Mazarin Stone
The Adventure of the Three Gables
The Adventure of the Sussex Vampire
The Adventure of the Three Garridebs
The Problem of Thor Bridge
The Adventure of the Creeping Man
The Adventure of the Lion's Mane
The Adventure of the Veiled Lodger
The Adventure of Shoscombe Old Place
The Adventure of the Retired Colourman

SCHOLARLY ABBREVIATIONS OF CASES

The constant use of the full name of each of the stories can make written discussions of the stories excessively lengthy. For this reason, the great American Sherlockian scholar, Jay Finley Christ, developed a system of coded abbreviations to represent each of the 60 stories in the Canon. This system has since been generally accepted by all those interested in the study of Sherlock Holmes. The coded abbreviations are as follows:

ABBE	The Abbey Grange	MUSG	The Musgrave Ritual
BERY	The Beryl Coronet	NAVA	The Naval Treaty
BLAC	Black Peter	NOBL	The Noble Bachelor
BLAN	The Blanched Soldier	NORW	The Norwood Builder
BLUE	The Blue Carbuncle	PREF	Preface to His Last Bow
BOSC	The Boscombe Valley Mystery	PRIO	The Priory School
BRUC	The Bruce-Partington Plans	REDC	The Red Circle
CARD	The Cardboard Box	REDH	The Red-Headed League
CHAS	Charles Augustus Milverton	REIG	The Reigate Squires
COPP	The Copper Beeches	RESI	The Resident Patient
CREE	The Creeping Man	RETI	The Retired Colourman
CROO	The Crooked Man	SCAN	A Scandal in Bohemia
DANC	The Dancing Men	SECO	The Second Stain
DEVI	The Devil's Foot	SHOS	Shoscombe Old Place
DYIN	The Dying Detective	SIGN	The Sign of Four
EMPT	The Empty House	SILV	Silver Blaze
ENGR	The Engineer's Thumb	SIXN	The Six Napoleons
FINA	The Final Problem	SOLI	The Solitary Cyclist
FIVE	The Five Orange Pips	SPEC	The Speckled Band
GLOR	The "Gloria Scott"	STOC	The Stock-Broker's Clerk
GOLD	The Golden Pince-Nez	STUD	A Study in Scarlet
GREE	The Greek Interpreter	SUSS	The Sussex Vampire
HOUN	The Hound of the Baskervilles	THOR	The Problem of Thor Bridge
IDEN	A Case of Identity	3GAB	The Three Gables
ILLU	The Illustrious Client	3GAR	The Three Garridebs
LADY	The Disappearance of Lady Frances Carfax	3STU	The Three Students
		TWIS	The Man with the Twisted Lip
LAST	His Last Bow	VALL	The Valley of Fear
LION	The Lion's Mane	VEIL	The Veiled Lodger
MAZA	The Mazarin Stone	WIST	Wisteria Lodge
MISS	The Missing Three-Quarter	YELL	The Yellow Face

ADDRESSES
Holmesian, Sherlockian and Doylean Societies

Actas de Baker Street
Bajada de la Plana 8
08032 Barcelona
Spain

The Baker Street Irregulars
(*Baker Street Journal* subscriptions only)
Fordham University Press
University Box L
Bronx
New York 10458–5172
USA

The Bootmakers of Toronto
420 Owen Sound Street
Shelburne
Ontario LON ISO
Canada

The Japan Sherlock Holmes Club
Ohizumi 2–55–8
Nerima
Tokyo 178
Japan

**The Registrar for SHERLOCK and
The Franco-Midland Hardware Company**
6 Bramham Moor
Hill Head
Fareham
Hampshire PO14 3RU
England

The Sherlock Holmes Society of Australia
PO Box 13
Stirling
South Australia 5152
Australia

The Sherlock Holmes Society of London
3 Outram Road
Southsea
Hampshire PO5 1QP
England

Sherlocktron
(Computerized bulletin board)
513 Via Presa
San Clemente
California 92672
USA

Von Herder Airguns Ltd
Berliner Strasse 6E
3005 Hemmingen
Germany

The Arthur Conan Doyle Society
"Grasmere"
35 Penfold Way
Dodleston
Chester CH4 9ML
England

A SELECTED HOLMESIAN
BIBLIOGRAPHY

Baring-Gould, H.S., *The Annotated Sherlock Holmes*, John Murray, London, 1968.

Baring-Gould, W.S., *Sherlock Holmes*, Rupert Hart-Davis, London, 1962.

Blakeney, T.S., *Sherlock Holmes: Fact or Fiction?*, John Murray, London, 1932.

Dakin, D.M., *A Sherlockian Commentary*, David & Charles, Newton Abbot, 1972.

Davis, D.S., *Holmes of the Movies*, New English Library, London, 1976.

De Waal, R., *The World Bibliography of Sherlock Holmes and Doctor Watson*, New York Graphic Society, New York, 1974.

De Waal, R., *The International Sherlock Holmes*, Mansell, London, 1980.

De Waal, R., *The Universal Sherlock Holmes*, Greenwood, Westport, CT, 1992.

Eyles, A., *Sherlock Holmes – A Centenary Celebration*, John Murray, London, 1986.

Folsom, H.T., *Through the Years at Baker Street*, Folsom, Randolph, 1991.

Green, R.L., *The Uncollected Sherlock Holmes*, Penguin, London, 1983.

Haining, P., *The Television Sherlock Holmes*, Virgin, London, 1991.

Hall, T.H., *Sherlock Holmes – Ten Literary Studies*, Duckworth, London, 1969.

McQueen, I., *Sherlock Holmes Detected*, David & Charles, Newton Abbot, 1974.

Redmond, D.A., *Sherlock Holmes – A Study in Sources*, McGill-Queen's University Press, Kingston & Montreal, 1982.

Shreffler, P.A. (Ed), *Baker Street Studies – Cornerstone Writings about Sherlock Holmes*, Greenwood Press, London, 1984.

Shreffler P.A. (Ed), *Sherlock Holmes By Gas-lamp*, Fordham University Press, New York, 1989.

Starrett, V., *The Private Life of Sherlock Holmes*, Allen & Unwin, London, 1961.

Steinbrunner C. and Michaels N., *The Films of Sherlock Holmes*, Citadel, Secaucus, 1978.

Tracey, J., *The Encyclopedia Sherlockiana*, Doubleday, New York, 1979.

Weller, P.L., *Elementary Holmes*, Sherlock Publications, Fareham, 1991.

It should be noted that many of these books are now out of print, but they are available through most major library networks.

INDEX

CONAN DOYLE CHARACTERS

DR. WATSON

ACKNOWLEDGEMENTS

British Telecom's permanent exhibition *The Story of Telecommunications*: 27 above; 28. Richard Lancelyn Green: 8; 11 left; 13 left, above; 14 far right; 15 left above; 16 right above, below, right; 17 below (courtesy ITC/Rank), far left; 18; 21 above; 29; 30; 32; 37; 38; 40 above centre (courtesy ITC/Rank), above right, below; 42 left, right; 43 above left; 45; 48; 50; 53; 55 left, above; 60; 61 left; 62; 65 left; 68 below; 69 left; 70 below; 71–88; 89 above, left; 90; 91 far left, left; 92; 95–97; 99; 101–109; 113; 114; 118; 125; 126; 127 above; 129 left below; 130 top; 131–136; 137 below. Stanley MacKenzie: 6; 10; 11 above; 12; 14 right, above; 15 above, left below; 16 above; 17 left; 19; 20 below; 25 below; 27 left; 31 below, left; 34; 36 below; 39 left; 40 left; 41; 42 below; 43 above right; 51 right, left, below; 52; 54; 55 left; 56; 57; 58 right, far right, below; 59 far left, left, near left; 60 right, right above; 64; 65 far left, below; 66; 67; 69 above; 89 far left; 90; 91 above, left below; 94; 99; 110; 111; 116; 120; 127 right; 128; 129 left; 130 above; 137 above. Metropolitan Police Museum: 23; 24; 25 right below, left below, above; 26; 46. National Portrait Gallery, London: 122. Sherlock Holmes Pub: 20 above; 21 left; 22; 35 left, above; 70 far right; 93. Philip Weller: 7; 21 left above; 36 above left, above; 39 above; 43 above; 58 right; 59 second row from top; 60 near right, top left, second row left, centre; 61 below; 68 above.

Special photography Andy Stewart.